Praise for *I'll Meet You There*

T0273204

A timely book with the growing rec~~o~~g............ ...., ~~p~~~~s~~~~y~~~~c~~~~h~~~~o~~~~l~~~~o~~~~gy~~, and business of the important function of empathy and the painful consequences of the lack of empathy. Shantigarbha shows the essential links between mindfulness, empathy, and compassion as expressions of a well-integrated heart and mind. This book is essential reading for those who wish to explore this important area of inner work.

Christopher Titmuss, Insight Meditation teacher, co-founder of Gaia House retreat centre

An excellent book on empathy that teases out the centrality of this value in Buddhism as the foundation for the cultivation of compassion and loving-kindness.

Stephen Batchelor, Buddhist teacher and author, co-founder of Sharpham College

Global social expansion has created a sense of urgency, cultivating conditions that have allowed mindlessness to thrive. Coupled with this is an increasing lack of empathy. The benefits of mindfulness and empathy are not just for societies but extend to communities, families and individuals. If mindfulness and empathy could be compared to medications, they would be seen as more effective than aspirin, which has been hailed as a 'wonder drug', and is prescribed in low doses as a way to prevent clots and strokes. This unassuming, inexpensive drug has been able to save millions of lives. The same is true of mindfulness and empathy. If more individuals engaged in cultivating awareness and empathy, the world as we know it would radically change. *I'll Meet You There* explains why empathy is a vital elixir needed by all. The author explains how empathy changes the brain at the neuron-synaptic level. I recommend this book to help deepen the discussion, explain the importance and strengthen the understanding of mindfulness and empathy in our daily lives.

Megrette Fletcher, author of *Discover Mindful Eating*, co-founder of The Center for Mindful Eating, TCME.org

In this comprehensive, well-researched book, Shantigarbha invites you to explore the topics of empathy and compassion through the lens of mindful awareness and empathic practice. Rich with examples and exercises, reading this book has inspired a vision of a world where compassion and empathic presence is embodied by all of humanity.

Sylvia Haskvitz, CNVC Certified Trainer, consultant and author, *Eat by Choice, Not by Habit*

I see Shantigarbha's study of empathy as a very welcome addition to a field of growing significance in all areas of life. Anyone who wants to understand this emerging discipline would benefit from the thorough research, wealth of information, conceptual clarity, and lively examples and exercises that this book contains.

Miki Kashtan, NVC Trainer and BayNVC.org co-founder

It is rare to find a book that both summarises scientific data and touches the reader in such a heartfelt way. Although this book is consistent with the scientific data it is also refreshingly unconstrained by it. Instead it synthesises scientific knowledge to date with age old wisdom from the Buddhist tradition. This approach allows for deeper exploration of empathy and compassion than science, which only scratches the surface. That the ideas expressed resonate so deeply is testament to the author's experiential & conceptual knowledge of empathy & mindfulness.

Dr Emma J Lawrence, former Lecturer in Cognition and Neuroimaging, Section of Cognitive Neuropsychiatry, Department of Psychological Medicine, Institute of Psychiatry, London, UK

I'll Meet You There is a wise, unique and beautifully written history of empathy and why empathy is important in experiencing compassion. This is a book for anyone who wants hope for living in a peaceful, humane world, and who wants a guide for how to get there.

Mary Mackenzie, author of *Peaceful Living: Daily Meditations for Living in Peace, Healing and Compassion*

I can wholeheartedly recommend this book. I enjoy the clarity, warmth and support I receive from your words. I appreciate the encouragement to live in the present and utilize every moment as an opportunity to deepen into connection and compassion. The encouragement is empowered by practices carefully crafted to awaken the nonviolence at the heart of our basic nature. The stories you weave humanize the practice and the practitioner, helping to fuel aspiration into integration. Thank you for all the energy and love you put into creating a resource likely to contribute to the awakening of our planet.

Jim Manske, NVC Trainer, Radicalcompassion.com

No matter how much I know about something there is always room for improvement. This is the same with empathy. Empathy cannot be learned from a book, BUT this book can definitely sharpen our knowledge and clarity about it. I highly recommend this book to everyone who cares about empathy, especially if you include this topic in your teaching.

Eva Rambala, NVC Trainer, coordinator and inspirer of NVC in Eastern Europe

Shantigarbha Warren weaves the connection of Empathy, Mindfulness, Neuroscience and NVC into a comfortable blanket that has the potential to warm the world.

Beverly Russo, educator

Shantigarbha Warren's book captures the essence of empathy, which serves to define it for the modern world and therefore make it relevant. Lacing empathy with the threads of Mindfulness, Neuroscience, and the practice of Nonviolent Communication, makes the concepts of the book actionable immediately to any who read it. The exercises at each chapter's end serve the purpose of mindfulness and bring the reader to a deeper level of understanding.

Mike Russo, high school administrator for at-risk youth, USA

Written with clarity and sensitivity, *I'll Meet You There* is clear-sighted in its approach to healing and transformation. I encourage all who pick up this book to read it cover to cover.

Claude AnShin Thomas, Zen Buddhist monk and author of *At Hell's Gate: A Soldier's Journey from War to Peace*

I'll Meet You There

A practical guide to empathy, mindfulness, and communication

Shantigarbha

indhorse Publications

Windhorse Publications
169 Mill Road
Cambridge
CB1 3AN
UK

info@windhorsepublications.com
windhorsepublications.com

Cover design by Katarzyna Manecka

Typesetting and layout by Ruth Rudd

Printed by Bell & Bain Ltd, Glasgow

British Library Cataloguing in Publication Data:
A catalogue record for this book is available from the British Library.

ISBN: 978-1-911407-41-6

Contents

List of figures

About the author

Shantigarbha is an experienced teacher of both Nonviolent Communication (NVC) and Buddhism. He studied classics and philosophy at Keble College, Oxford, before devoting himself full-time to following the Buddha's teachings. He was ordained into the Triratna Buddhist Order in 1996 and given the name Shantigarbha, which means 'Seed or Womb of Peace'. Through his Buddhist practice, he came across NVC and has been sharing it as a certified trainer since 2004.

He is a trainer on the Centre for Nonviolent Communication's International Intensive Trainings, and is an assessor-in-training for South Asia. In 2012 he ran a reconciliation retreat with a team of NVC trainers including Sylvia Haskvitz for 100 Israelis and Palestinians near the Dead Sea. In 2015 he devised and co-led a reconciliation event between ex-Maoist combatants, 'victims', and government officials in Nepal, which became the subject of the documentary 'In the eyes of the good'.

Within the Triratna Buddhist Community, he currently serves as the secretary of the Triratna Trust and the UK and Ireland Order delegate to the Triratna International Council.

For more information about Shantigarbha and his Nonviolent Communication activities, visit his website at SeedofPeace.org.

Gratitude

Thank you to my Buddhist teachers, especially Urgyen Sangharakshita, who founded the Triratna Buddhist Order. He introduced me to the riches of the Buddhist tradition and set an example of how to live according to its principles. I'm also grateful to Marshall Rosenberg, developer of Nonviolent Communication,[1] who showed me how to embody empathy and compassion in my speech. I'm grateful to Megrette Fletcher, who commented on early drafts of this book; Emma Lawrence, who set me straight on the neuroscience of empathy; and Stephen Batchelor, who pointed out additional Buddhist references. Finally, I'm grateful to my partner Gesine, family, and friends for their enduring love and support.

Publisher's acknowledgements

Windhorse Publications wishes
to gratefully acknowledge
a grant from the Triratna
European Chairs' Assembly
Fund and the Future Dharma
Fund towards the production of
this book.

We also wish to
acknowledge and thank the
individual donors who gave to
the book's production via our
'Sponsor-a-book' campaign.

Audio downloads

This book has been produced with accompanying guided meditations and reflections by the author, available as free downloads. They are marked with a 🧘, and can be streamed directly from the Web or downloaded in MP3 format. Please go to bit.ly/MeetYouThereAudio or windhorsepublications.com/meet-you-there-audio/

Out beyond ideas of wrongdoing and rightdoing,
there is a field. I'll meet you there.

When the soul lies down in that grass,
the world is too full to talk about.
Ideas, language, even the phrase, each other
doesn't make any sense.

– Jalaluddin Rumi[2]

Introduction

We get connected with each other in the space that opens up when we let go of our ideas of good and bad, right and wrong. When we feel safe and connected to ourselves, we don't need to use these labels. When we are connected to ourselves, we are also connected to the people around us.

It's hard to find words to describe this field. In a sense it is beyond words. We are connected in such a way that it hardly makes sense to talk about us as separate beings. There's just a sense of compassionate presence, intense closeness, and empathy. *I'll meet you there.* That's where I want to live my life. Through empathy we can find a way to stay connected to our humanity and to contribute to a more peaceful world.

It's also important that we know some steps towards Rumi's field, the place where we feel safe and connected with ourselves and each other.

Part 1, 'A brief history of empathy', is a whistle-stop tour from evolutionary times to the present, taking in the Buddha and Jesus, the origins of the word 'empathy', and modern psychological research.

Part 2, 'Empathy and Nonviolent Communication (NVC)', introduces Marshall Rosenberg, developer of Nonviolent Communication, and takes you through the practical skills of how to empathize, culminating in empathy archery.

Part 3, 'A Buddhist perspective', explores how empathy is a fundamental part of this spiritual tradition.

Part 4, 'Drawing the threads together', looks at the development of empathy in children and the relation between empathy and compassion.

To empathize with others, we need to learn how to empathize with ourselves, so that, when we reach out, we do so *from the inside out*. To support this, in each chapter there are practical exercises for individual or group study.

Part 1

A brief history of empathy

When we hear another person's feelings and needs,
we recognize our common humanity.

– Marshall Rosenberg[1]

Chapter one

....

The evolution of empathy

During his long career as an international peacemaker, Marshall Rosenberg was once asked to help mediate a conflict between two tribes in northern Nigeria. The conflict had arisen over how many locations each tribe would have to display its wares in the marketplace. There were 400 people in the community. One hundred of them had been killed over this dispute in the preceding year. A colleague of Marshall's had worked hard for six months with the chiefs on both sides to get them to agree to meet. As Marshall walked into the room his colleague warned him, 'Be prepared for some tension, Marshall. Three of the people who are going to be in the meeting know that someone who killed their child is in the room.'

Twelve chiefs from the Christian tribe sat on one side of the table, and twelve chiefs from the Muslim tribe sat on the other. Marshall and his colleague sat in between. Marshall began with a question that's central to his Nonviolent Communication process, 'I'd like whoever wants to tell me: what needs of yours are not being met in this conflict? I'm confident that, if you can all hear one another's needs, we can find strategies for meeting everyone's needs.'

Immediately a chief from the Christian tribe screamed across the table, 'You people are murderers.' A chief from the Muslim tribe screamed back, 'You people have been trying to dominate us for eighty years.' This was no surprise to Marshall. He asked for needs and got a diagnosis of the other side's pathology – intellectual judgements justifying a position. Hearing these kinds of 'enemy images', it was easy for him to understand why 30 per cent of the population had been killed over the question of places in the marketplace. The chiefs were screaming at each other, and it wasn't easy to re-establish order. He realized that he was going to have to work hard to help the chiefs translate their enemy images into unmet needs.

As a mediator, he was working on the assumption that all criticism, blame, and enemy images are a tragic expression of the speaker's *own* needs. Beneath 'You people are murderers', it wasn't hard for him to guess that the need was for safety. So Marshall said, 'Chief, are you saying that your need for safety isn't met by how things are being dealt with? You would hope that, no matter what's going on, things would be resolved with nonviolence, correct?' He heard the need behind the analysis. If his guess had been inaccurate, the speaker could have helped him. On this occasion Marshall guessed accurately. The Christian chief was shocked, because he wasn't used to talking from inside, where his needs were. He was used to calling people names. However, after reflecting, he said, 'That's exactly what I'm saying.'

Now Marshall had to be sure that the chief's need was heard by the other side. So he asked the chiefs from the other tribe, 'Chiefs, is there one of you who is willing to reflect back what the chief from the first tribe said his needs were?' He did this so that they could see another human being like them. Of course they were in too much pain to empathize, so one of them screamed, 'Then why did you kill my son?'

Marshall knew that it wouldn't be easy, even once he had got the Christian chief to express his needs, to get the other side to see his humanness. He knew that enemy images were in the way. It's not easy to empathize, even if it's a simple message, if the other side's brain has been programmed to diagnose pathology. So Marshall said, 'Chief, we'll come to that issue soon. For the moment, could you tell me what the first chief's needs are?' His second response was, 'You can't trust these people, they'll say anything.' So Marshall repeated, 'This person says he has a need for safety. Tell me, Chief, what did you hear him say? Could you just repeat that, Chief, so I'm sure we're communicating?' It took three or four times of asking before he was able to hear this simple phrase. But eventually the second chief said, 'The man says that he has a need for safety that isn't being met by the way some of the conflicts are being dealt with.'

Even though it had taken a lot of effort, Marshall was delighted. By acknowledging the first chief's need, the second chief had empathized with him – he had seen his humanness. We see humanness by seeing the needs of others without enemy images clouding them. Marshall knew that it wasn't easy to do that, especially in such an emotionally charged situation. It required full presence to what was alive in the other person. But that first step had been taken. They were now out of intellectual analysis in order to justify positions, and connecting at the level of human needs.

Marshall helped the other chiefs of the first side express their needs. Once they had been heard, he turned to the chiefs of the second side and said, 'Now that you hear what the needs of the other side are, I'd like you to tell me your needs.' The chief who had spoken earlier repeated his judgement, 'They have been trying to dominate us for a long time, and we're not going to put up with it any more.' Marshall translated this judgement of wrongness on the part of the other side into the needs he sensed at the root of this judgement, by asking, 'Are you upset because you have a strong need for equality in this community?' The chief said, 'Yes.' Marshall turned to a member of the other tribe and asked, 'Could you repeat that, so I'm sure we're communicating?' They weren't able to do it at first. Marshall had to repeat the message at least twice before they were able to acknowledge the other side's need.

This all took about an hour, because there was a lot of yelling and confusion. At that point, one of the chiefs who hadn't said anything jumped up and spoke in an impassioned way. He'd seen the change in the atmosphere in the room, from calling names to seeing what everybody's needs were, and said, 'If we know how to speak in this way we don't have to kill each other.' Marshall later commented, 'It didn't take long for this chief to see that, if we can just talk about our needs, and not get into an analysis of who's right and who's wrong, we can solve anything.'[2]

Marshall's claim seems hard to believe in a world where we have 'terrorists' broadcasting public beheadings, and an international 'war on terror' that uses 'terror' tactics like drone strikes to achieve its aims. The world is shrinking. We hear more and more about conflicts and problems in other countries, and how the actions of groups and states in one region affect people thousands of miles away. The prevailing popular narrative is that you can't talk to terrorists – you can only 'show 'em', that is, defeat violence with violence. We ignore that this often leads to an escalation of violence. There are a few exceptions, of course: the Northern Ireland peace process, or Nelson Mandela's almost single-handed political integration of blacks and whites in South Africa. But the prevailing myth played out in movie theatres across the Western world is that you fight terror with greater terror.

Marshall's experience told him differently. He'd trained himself to empathize, to put his attention on the humanness of both sides, rather than what divides them. In my career as a mediator, I've tried to emulate this. Sometimes I can see people's humanness, and sometimes my own judgements get in the way. One of the first mediations I did was with a young, unmarried, professional couple in London. Rachel and Paul had been going through difficulties. I told them that I wasn't going to take sides, and made a proposal about my role ... if I heard something that was likely to be heard as blame or criticism, I would translate it and check to see if my translation was accurate. They agreed.

At first things seemed to be going well, and they were both eager to let the other talk. But eventually Rachel got round to talking about the time they spent together in the evenings: 'When we go out for meals, you always look bored or tired', she said. And then she raised her voice and looked directly at him, 'You never listen to me!'

I could see Paul stiffening up, so I asked him, 'Could you tell me what need you heard Rachel expressing?'

He paused for a moment and said with a sigh, 'She thinks I never listen to her.'

I felt stuck with this, because he hadn't told me a need. But I picked myself up and said, 'Thank you for telling me what she thinks. What need was she expressing?'

'I'm new to this', he said. 'Could you help me?'

'Okay,' I said, taking this as a cue that he wanted to borrow my empathic skills, 'what I heard was this – she needs to be fully heard and understood.'

'Oh', said Paul, looking down.

'What do you hear now?'

'She doesn't feel heard and understood.'

I looked at Rachel. She nodded, then sat back in her chair, relaxed.

I felt relieved that Rachel had been heard, but also nervous, as Paul was still looking down, unmoved. Some pain had been stirred up in him. I wasn't confident that he would be able to connect with his needs, so I took my heart in my hands and guessed, 'Does that stir up some pain for you? Would you like acknowledgement of the energy you put into this relationship?'

'Yes', he said, looking up at me with surprise and relief.

I turned to Rachel, 'Could you tell me what you heard me say?'

'He's just trying to get out of it', she replied angrily. 'He always turns it back on me.'

It was hard for me to stay calm. I thought, what's wrong with her. He's listened to her. The least she can do is return the favour. But no, she's still got to attack ... no wonder he's thinking about leaving her... I took a breath and connected with myself... I really wanted them both to experience the relief of being heard. I said, 'That wasn't what I meant. I was asking you to repeat my guess of his feelings and needs. Could you do that?'

'Oh, you mean he's hurt because he wants recognition for the energy he puts into the relationship.'

'Yes, that's what I heard.' I heard Paul breathing out a sigh and sitting back in his chair.

I felt elated: both of them had now been heard. But I guessed that Rachel was still holding a need for balance or fairness in the relationship. I asked her about this, and she said she agreed. With this, something seemed to settle in her, and she started looking shyly at Paul. Feeling playful, I said, 'Let's see what we can do to give Paul some acknowledgement. Rachel, could you tell Paul three things he does that you do enjoy?'

'Three things?' said Rachel, laughing.

'Yes,' said Paul, 'that would be nice.'

Rachel was silent for a moment then started to tell him about the times she enjoyed being with him and what she loved about him.

Seeing them move closer, I went out to make a cup of tea and left them to it.

The evolution of empathy

These stories illustrate the power of empathy to create connection. But where does the story of empathy start? Renowned Dutch-American zoologist Frans de Waal believes that it is part of our evolutionary heritage. He claims that it goes back at least 100 million years, to when humans were first group-living mammals. De Waal spent a lifetime studying the social behaviour of primates, including empathy and conflict resolution. He gathered evidence from various fields and combined it with his own studies on primates to argue that humans are group animals – highly cooperative, sometimes warlike, but mostly peace-loving.[3]

The picture we usually get from Darwinism is that humans are competitive and aggressive. Of course there is some truth to this. However, we are also intensely social. Empathy is part of our evolution – not just a recent part, but an age-old capacity. Human babies empathize from day one. It's not as complex a skill as it has been made out to be. It doesn't rely on more advanced skills, such as the ability to 'see things through another person's eyes'. In its most primitive and ancient form, empathy relies on emotional contagion.

Have you noticed how a mood can pass quickly through a crowd without anything being said? Psychologists call this emotional contagion. Emotions are contagious. In the lab, studies have shown that people tend to imitate other people's expressions of pain, laughter, smiling, and so on. Emotional contagion in turn rests on the even more primitive capacities of body-mapping and imitation.

Body-mapping is the automatic impulse to move the same part of your body as you see moving. It starts early in the life of mammals. An adult coos and sticks her tongue out at a newborn human baby. The baby will respond in kind by sticking its tongue out. For apes and monkeys, it is the same: they will mimic a researcher slowly opening and closing his mouth. Imitation is the tendency to adopt the situation, emotions, and behaviour of those you are close to. Children often imitate the way their parent walks, dresses, and speaks. This is also seen in apes – in fact the phrase 'to ape' means to copy another's movements. There are countless experimental examples of apes imitating each other, learning new skills. Body-mapping and imitation are the basic building blocks of social connection and bonding in mammals.[4]

Emotional contagion is more than just imitation. When you mimic the expressions, sounds, postures, and movements of another person, *you tend to feel what they are feeling*. Experimentally it's been found in both humans and animals. What's remarkable about emotional contagion is that it's not a choice. You don't decide to mimic and feel what the other person is feeling, you just do it automatically. To test this, Swedish researchers stuck small electrodes onto people's faces to register the tiniest muscle movements of frowning and smiling. Pictures of angry and happy faces appeared on a computer screen. As expected, the participants frowned in reaction to angry faces and smiled in reaction to happy ones.

However, the researchers argued that the participants could have *decided* to respond in this way. To test for this, they flashed pictures of angry and happy faces too quickly to be seen consciously. Amazingly, there was the same reaction. The participants had no awareness of seeing angry or happy faces, but the muscles in their faces still mimicked them. Even more surprisingly, these flashing images induced emotions. The participants who had been shown happy faces reported feeling better than the ones who'd seen angry faces. This means that the researchers were observing and recording genuine emotional contagion – emotional face-to-face communication occurring on an unconscious level.[5]

This primitive form of empathy probably goes back 200 million years to the birth of parental care. It had immense evolutionary benefit. Mammalian mothers who were more sensitive to their babies' needs were more successful in keeping them alive. It probably also emerged in another context: the way mammals mate and form a pair. Sharing food with a partner required a larger, more powerful brain, and probably acted as a driver for the emergence of emotional contagion.[6]

It's not just humans who have the capacity for emotional contagion. Researchers have found it in apes and monkeys, and even mice have been found to be sensitive to another mouse's pain. The Swedish experiments show that this primitive form of empathy isn't an intellectual process of imagining another's situation. They also suggest that full empathy isn't driven by the capacity to imagine another's experience, but by *emotional engagement*. Emotional engagement is produced by face-to-face connections such as seeing the other's face and hearing their voice.

But the evolution of empathy didn't stop with emotional contagion. On the basis of emotional contagion developed the capacity to be actively concerned for others. Concern for others can appear as consolation for a loser, as when someone gently touches or sits with the loser in a fight. It can also appear as altruistic activity, as when a younger member of a group helps an unrelated arthritic elder to find a seat. These forms of concern for others are well-established parts of human social life. Like emotional contagion, they aren't restricted to humans. Studies have repeatedly found these forms of social behaviour in apes, and they are very likely to be found in dolphins and whales. Perhaps it's not surprising – they have obvious evolutionary benefits for animals that live in groups, being part of the social glue that keeps groups together.

Finally and most recently in the evolution of empathy comes the ability to take another's perspective. Perspective-taking is a clear understanding of the other's needs in a particular situation. This is properly seeing things through another person's eyes. It allows us to help each other in a specific and appropriate way.

Imagine coming across a lone child in a crowd. The child is looking from side to side and calling for her mummy. You might feel concerned. You can imagine that she's scared and she

I'll Meet You There

wants to be safe. Perhaps you go towards the child and make eye contact with her. But then you evaluate your options. Does anyone else know about the situation? Does the child look blue in the face – a sign that she is suffering from cold? Does she have enough presence of mind to tell you her name? Where did she most likely come from? Might her mother be in a nearby shop? If you listen, can you hear a woman calling? Is there an obvious place where her mother might go to look?

Perspective-taking is a combination of two factors – getting aroused emotionally and seeing things through another's eyes. The emotional arousal makes you care, and the cognitive approach helps you appraise the situation. These two sides need to be in balance. If you are over-aroused (overwhelmed, panicky, or distressed), you may lose your ability to take the other's perspective and help in a targeted way. If you see the child and panic with them, you won't be able to form a rational plan to help them.

But there is another factor at play here. Perspective-taking seems to depend on a sense of self. It's the complex process of taking another's perspective and separating yourself enough from it to appraise the situation. Again, perspective-taking and helping in an appropriate way are not restricted to humans. Researchers have found that apes and elephants are capable of these forms of social behaviour. They are also likely to be found in other large-brained animals such as dolphins and whales. The cut-off line seems to come between apes, who have larger brains, and their smaller-brained monkey cousins. Monkeys lack a sense of self except in a rudimentary form.

Researchers have witnessed this inability of monkeys. A troupe of monkeys is moving across a landscape and encounters a stream. The adults go ahead and jump the stream, but one of the youngsters hangs back and hesitates. One of the adult monkeys looks back and picks up on the youngster's distress. He may even feel concern for the youngster. But if *he* can jump the stream, the adult assumes that *everyone* can do it. He can't make the imaginative leap of realizing that not everyone has the same strength, agility, and confidence as him. So he will be unable to help in an appropriate way, for instance by standing in the stream to show how deep it is, or leading the youngster to a place where it's easier to cross. He remains standing, looking back, puzzled why the youngster doesn't jump, lacking the cognitive ability to figure out what the youngster needs.

Perspective-taking is the most recent and advanced layer of empathy, and allows us to help others in an appropriate way. In the past, some writers have claimed that empathy is the one truly *human* quality that differentiates humans from other animals. Now the boundary seems vaguer than before. Humans have a more developed capacity for empathy and self-awareness than animals. We can more easily take another's perspective, and we seem to be the only species that can generalize empathy towards groups and classes, for instance endangered species. Despite this, the difference between humans' and animals' ability to empathize seems to be a matter of degree, not kind.

Seeing the humanity of others comes with practice. In the following exercise you can start to train your empathy muscles by taking Ceri's perspective as she waits in a coffee shop for her friend Bernice to arrive.

 Empathy exercise

- Purpose of this activity: to see the humanness of others by seeing their needs
- Tools: a notepad or journal and a pencil
- Time: 5 minutes

Try to guess Ceri's needs below. Look at each of the sentences in italics and guess the needs behind Ceri's words. If you want, you can compare your guesses with mine. However, bear in mind that there are no 'right' answers. As Marshall Rosenberg said, 'You can't guess wrong, only human.'

'I got there about 11:25. I remember because *we agreed to meet at 11:30* and I checked my phone when I arrived. It was our usual meeting place – a coffee shop along the Gloucester Road. *I got myself a coffee at the counter and settled into a comfy armchair. Bernice was often a bit late.* When it got to 11:40 I started to wonder where she was. Had she got held up in traffic? Or waylaid in a shop somewhere? *I tried to call her, but her phone was switched off.* I didn't leave a voicemail – she never checks them. Now I was a bit worried, and also a bit annoyed. Why was she always late for our appointments? *She didn't seem to care about our time.* It's not as if we met that often. Perhaps she found me rather boring. After all, she'd moved on from where we used to live, got a good job, a nice house. Perhaps I just pulled her down. I started thinking about my own life. Had I really made a success of it? *Or was I just making do with whatever crumbs other people left me?* I started to feel quite dejected, sitting there. When she finally breezed in at 11:55, *I didn't know whether to smile or cry.'*

My guesses of Ceri's needs

We agreed to meet at 11:30. Initially I sense that Ceri enjoys reliability and honouring agreements, and is looking forward to some friendly connection.

I got myself a coffee at the counter and settled into a comfy armchair. Bernice was often a bit late. There's some acceptance that her friend is often late, so Ceri finds ways to comfort herself.

I tried to call her, but her phone was switched off. Ceri is seeking clarity and wants to make sure that Bernice is okay (needs for care and safety).

She didn't seem to care about our time. Now Ceri's need to be valued is coming up.

Or was I just making do with whatever crumbs other people left me? Ceri wants to value herself, and find meaning and purpose in life. I also sense echoes of other needs: creativity, mastery, to contribute to life.

How did you get on?

Do unto others as you would have them do unto you.

– St Luke's Gospel[1]

Chapter two

....

The Buddha and Jesus

Our timescale now shortens from millions of years of evolution to the last two or three thousand years. Exploring the historical record, we find empathy in the life of Gautama the Buddha. He was born in the foothills of the Himalayas, in what is now southern Nepal, and died around 400 BCE.[2] His father was the elected chief of the Śākyan tribal confederacy.[3] He was given the name Siddhattha, and as a young man he left home and wandered south to the vast plains of the Ganges. It was there that he gained Enlightenment and spread his teachings. The story of how he came to leave home is told in the 'four sights'.[4] It contains legendary or mythical elements that reflect the world view of the time, which would be out of place in a strictly historical biography.

We're told that the young Siddhattha lived a life of extreme refinement, away from pain and hardship. He had three beautiful palaces, one for each season.[5] His father Suddhodana wanted his sensitive son to grow up to be a great king. He was afraid that, if Siddhattha saw suffering, he might leave home to become a wandering truth-seeker, so he made sure that his son only saw beauty and youth.

But Siddhattha wanted to leave the palace to visit the royal gardens, so he climbed into his chariot and set out. The local devas (gods) decided to lend a helping hand, and put an old man by the side of the road. The man had grey hair and no teeth, his back was bent, and he could only walk with a stick. Siddhattha said to his charioteer, 'That man isn't like other people. What do you call him?' His charioteer replied, 'Your Majesty, he is an old man.' Siddhattha, who had never seen an old person before, asked, 'What does "old man" mean?' The charioteer replied, 'An old man is someone who has only a short time to live.' The prince asked, 'Am I also subject to old age? Can I not avoid it?' The charioteer told him, 'Your Majesty, we're all subject to old age. No one can avoid it.' Siddhattha was shocked by this and said, 'If all human beings are liable to old age, including me, I'm not interested in the royal gardens any more! Turn the chariot round and drive back to the palace.'

Back in the palace, the prince became gloomy and dejected. The fearful king tried to distract him with female attendants and dancing girls. For a while this worked, but later Siddhattha rode out again to see the royal gardens. His father put soldiers on the road to conceal any kind of unpleasantness, but this time the local devas made a sick man appear by the roadside. The sick man appeared to be in great pain, suffering from disease, and could only sit up with help. Again the prince wondered what this was. Again, the charioteer told him, 'A sick man doesn't know if he will recover from his illness. All of us, your Majesty, are prone to sickness.' Siddhattha lost his desire to see the gardens and turned back to the palace.

Later the prince rode out for a third time. Suddhodana doubled the guard on the road, but this time Siddhattha saw the corpse of a dead man, lying on a stretcher and surrounded by mourners. Horrified, he asked, 'What is a dead man?' His charioteer replied, 'Your Majesty, his relatives will never see him again, nor will he see his relatives. We are all subject to death. None of us can overcome it, even you, your Majesty.' Siddhattha said, 'If all human beings are subject to death, I don't want to see the gardens any more. Take me back to the palace.'

Looking at the first three sights, it's clear that Siddhattha had a kind of empathic realization. He realized, 'If it can happen to them, it can happen to me.' We don't need to believe the story literally, that he had never seen the old, the sick, or the dead before. We can take it symbolically as a process that everyone goes through. At some point we see the facts of life *as if for the first time*, and then it hits us. We're all subject to old age, sickness, and death. We see ourselves in others, and there is a corresponding growth in self-awareness.

The story suggests that this process isn't going to be easy... Siddhattha gets depressed. For a while he doesn't enjoy the pleasures available to him. Then he gradually forgets and goes back to pleasure-seeking without any deeper meaning. How many times has this happened to us? But over time, awareness of reality cuts deeper, and he becomes ready to see a fourth sight.

A few months later, the prince had again forgotten the previous sights. Riding out in his royal chariot, he saw a bald-headed man dressed in ragged robes. The charioteer told him that this was a wanderer, someone who had left home to seek the truth. Siddhattha was curious to find out more, and went to speak to him. He admired the man for changing his life and committing himself to seeking the truth. In time Siddhattha copied him, leaving home to seek salvation.

A vision of lotus flowers

Siddhattha's spiritual experiences culminated in his Enlighten-ment at the age of thirty-five. But immediately afterwards he faced a dilemma. When he reflected on the profound truth he had discovered, he realized that it was going to be difficult to communicate. In fact, people were so caught up in the stories they told themselves about the world that, even if he did share his experience, they wouldn't understand. The Buddha was inclined not to share what he had discovered.[6] But fortunately the story doesn't end there. According to the legendary account, a great god named Brahma Sahampati, Lord of the Thousand Worlds, read the Buddha's mind. Brahma Sahampati realized that, if the Buddha didn't share what he had discovered, the world would be lost. So he went to talk to the Buddha. We can imagine Gautama the Buddha sitting peacefully under the bodhi tree, and Brahma Sahampati approaching him like a great golden light. After bowing to the Buddha and saluting him with folded hands, Brahma Sahampati begged him to teach: 'Let the Blessed One teach the Dharma. There are beings in the world who haven't heard the truth yet. There are those who aren't fulfilling their potential because of this.' He rounded off, 'Open the doors to the Deathless! There will be those who will understand.'

The Buddha reassessed the situation: 'Out of compassion for beings, I surveyed the world with the eye of a Buddha.' He saw that there were some beings who had 'little dust' in their eyes – who could learn and understand. It seemed to him that beings were like blue, red, and white lotus flowers growing in a pond. All of them were growing from the mud at the bottom. Some lived and thrived in the water without rising out of it, some rested on the surface, and some had risen out of the water. When he saw beings in this way, in terms of their spiritual potential, the Buddha was moved to compassion and decided to communicate what he had discovered:

> Open for them are the doors to the Deathless,
> Let those with ears now show their faith.[7]

Brahma Sahampati was satisfied with this, so he bowed to the Buddha and left.

In some ways this is a surprising story. We may imagine the Buddha as a perfect, desireless being. But immediately after his Enlightenment, he reveals a surprisingly human side. He doesn't want to teach, nobody will understand him, it will be tiring and troublesome. However, this isn't the only incident that shows the Buddha longing for a bit of peace and quiet. Many years later at Kosambi the Buddha tries to mediate between some quarrelling monks and fails, so he goes off to the forest to meditate. Touchingly, he's looked after by a bull elephant that has also left its herd to find peace.[8]

But back to Brahma Sahampati. Brahma Sahampati is supposedly the greatest god in the universe. He picks up on the Buddha's reluctance to teach and comes to plead with him. In a bizarre reversal of roles, the Lord of the Thousand Worlds visits someone sitting at the foot of a tree to beg him to change his mind. Brahma Sahampati argues that some beings will understand. The Buddha reassesses the situation. He looks out over the world with the 'Buddha-eye', the eye of intuitive insight that opened during his Enlightenment, and has a vision of beings as beautiful lotus flowers. All began life in the mud; all are at different stages of growth and development. All are trying to fulfil their life potential.

If the Buddha only took account of his wish for peace and ease, he wouldn't teach. But when he empathically connects with the potential of all beings for growth and development, something shifts deep inside him. He realizes that his deepest wish is to contribute to the world, to make a difference. There is no contradiction here: all humans have these different drives and longings. It is a powerful reminder of the need to contribute to the world, which is perhaps humanity's deepest need. The Buddha decides to share the truth he has discovered, to open the doors of the Deathless (nirvana or Enlightenment). Anyone who is prepared to make an effort may enter, as is anyone who is prepared to 'show their faith'.

At first the new Buddha connects with himself, wanting to enjoy his newfound transcendental peace and ease. This is a process of self-empathy that is known in psychology as self-compassion. Then the Buddha surveys the world with the eye of a Buddha. This is the process of imaginative identification with others that we know as empathy. Out of empathy arises compassion.

But what is compassion? According to the dictionary, it has two elements: a 'sympathetic consciousness' of others' pain, together with a desire to alleviate it. The sympathetic consciousness is empathy. The desire to reduce the pain is the element that transforms empathy into compassion.

In the Buddhist tradition, compassion is usually paired with wisdom; they are said to be the two aspects of Enlightenment. Compassion extends to include all sentient beings. It is only action that springs from wisdom that is truly compassionate. Coming back to the story, it's now possible to see more clearly the difference between empathy and compassion. Empathy is the vision of beings as lotuses: the emotional and imaginative identification with them, the sympathetic consciousness of others' pain. Compassion is the action part: the Buddha's decision to teach the truth he has discovered, the desire to alleviate suffering.

One final point: it is clear from the story that empathy is the aspect of compassion that reaches out to meet others *where they are* rather than where we would like them to be. This is a profound reminder. It's easy to be compassionate and kind in a generic way without really imagining what it's like being another person. Empathy personalizes compassion and gives it real traction.

Whether or not we're ready to alleviate suffering, we can reach out to beings where they are. We can create compassionate connection. This aspect of compassion was brought out by Marshall Rosenberg in the Nonviolent Communication (NVC) process he developed. As a child living in Detroit during the race riots of 1943, he saw violence and murder in the streets. Indoors, he watched his uncle caring lovingly for his paralyzed grandmother. Reflecting on these extremes, Rosenberg asked himself, 'What supports humans to be compassionate?' Later, he expressed his aspiration: 'What I want in my life is compassion, a flow between myself and others based on a mutual giving from the heart.'[9] By keeping our focus on this intention, we can stay compassionately connected to ourselves and others, even when there's conflict.

Actions have consequences

Another episode in the life of the Buddha illustrates his empathic concern for all creatures. It also shows his understanding of child psychology. One morning the Buddha was on his alms round, walking from door to door in the village with his begging bowl. He came across a gang of boys tormenting a crow with a broken wing. They seemed to be enjoying the 'fun'. The Buddha went over and asked the boys, 'If you get hit, does it hurt?' 'Yes,' they replied, 'it hurts.' The Buddha said, 'Well, when you hit that crow, it also feels hurt. You know how unpleasant it is to feel hurt, so why do you hurt another creature?' The boys thought about this for a moment, then put down their sticks and went away to find another game.[10]

What is remarkable about this story is what the Buddha *didn't* say. He didn't shout, 'Stop tormenting that crow!' And he didn't say, 'You're bad boys. Only bad boys torment crows.' Instead, he asked them to compare their own experience with that of the crow. Perhaps this was the first time in their lives that they stopped to do this. The text doesn't say how old the boys were. Perhaps they were only just developing the self-awareness that would enable them to imagine the crow's experience.

Asking questions, rather than making moralistic judgements or giving commands, is an 'inductive' approach to teaching. It is in strong contrast to power-over teaching methods that enforce rules and punishments. Modern research suggests that inductive techniques encourage children to think about the effect of their actions on others. And this in turn aids the development of empathy.[11]

In the Buddhist tradition, awareness of the impact of your actions on others is synonymous with ethical sensitivity. One of Urgyen Sangharakshita's teachers was a Tibetan lama called Dhardo Rimpoche. In the 1950s he set up a school in northern India for the children of Tibetan refugees. I had the honour to meet him at his school in 1988. After experience with generations of children, he was asked if he had any advice for parents in the West. He replied, 'They should teach their children that actions have consequences.'[12]

The golden rule: 'Do unto others...'

The golden rule encapsulates the ethics of empathy. What's good for you is also likely to be good for the people around you. Conversely, what's not good for you is also likely not to be good for others. The rule is best known from St Luke's Gospel: 'Do unto others as you would have them do unto you.' It first appeared in this form in a sixteenth-century Catholic catechism. In the catechism, it is given central importance as a *summary* of the ten commandments.[13]

The golden rule can be expressed both positively – 'Do to others what you would like to be done to you' – and negatively – 'Do not do to others what you would not like to be done to you.' Historically, the rule appears in various forms in the writings of ancient Egypt, ancient Greece, the Baha'i faith, Buddhism, Confucianism, Hinduism, Islam, Jainism, Judaism, Sikhism, and Taoism. It appeared most recently in 2008, when Karen Armstrong won the TED Prize for her dream to create a charter for compassion, newly enshrining the golden rule. Thousands of people contributed to the process and the charter was unveiled in November 2009. The charter states that 'The principle of compassion lies at the heart of all religious, ethical and spiritual traditions, calling us always to treat all others as we wish to be treated ourselves.' The charter has inspired community-based acts of compassion all over the world.[14]

The golden rule is a useful rule of thumb. However, it has limitations: it isn't flexible enough for all situations. What if the other person clearly has different priorities and values, even a different world view from you? The Irish writer and thinker George Bernard Shaw considered this. He suggested a witty alternative: 'Do not do unto others as you would that they should do unto you. Their tastes may not be the same.'[15] There is a serious point here: if others don't share your values, the way you want to be treated will be different from the way they want to be treated. The ethics of empathy might offer us a more sensitive guideline to acting compassionately.

The Good Samaritan

Coming into more recent biblical times, St Luke's Gospel describes an incident in which Jesus was tested by an expert in religious law.[16] The expert claimed that he had understood the importance of the ancient saying, 'Love your neighbour as yourself.'[17] Jesus approves of this, saying that the expert 'will inherit eternal life'. 'Love your neighbour as yourself' implies a principle of mutuality that is necessary for empathy to take place. Just as you enjoy the experience of being loved, so do your neighbours.

But the expert in religious law wants to test Jesus, so he asks, 'Who should I treat as my neighbour?' He wants to know how far Jesus extends his compassion. Jesus replies with the parable of the Good Samaritan. The parable clarifies that his principle of mutuality holds good even for a member of an outcast tribe. According to Jesus, your neighbours include even your most hated enemy.[18]

A Jewish man was travelling from the city of Jerusalem on the road that leads down towards the Dead Sea and Jericho when he was attacked by bandits. They stole his clothes, beat him up, and left him for dead at the side of the road. A Jewish priest came along, but, when he saw the man all naked and bloody, he crossed over to the other side. Later a Jewish temple assistant walked over to look at the man, but left him lying there. Then one of the tribe of despised Samaritans came along. When he saw the man lying there, he was moved to compassion. Instead of walking past, he treated the man's wounds and bandaged them. Next he put him on his donkey and took him to an inn, where he took care of him. The next day he gave the innkeeper two silver coins and said, 'Take care of this man. If it costs more than this, I'll pay you next time.' Jesus asked the expert in religious law, 'Now who was the real neighbour of the man who was attacked by bandits?'

The parable is primarily concerned with acting compassionately towards all, even one's enemies. But it implies empathy in other ways. Jesus assumes that his Jewish audience will empathize with the Jewish man attacked by bandits. And the story illustrates the capacity of all human beings to empathize with those outside of their tribe and religion.

By telling this particular version of the parable, Jesus gives a triple twist to 'Love your neighbour as yourself.' His audience might have expected a story about how a virtuous Jewish man (perhaps a priest) helped a Samaritan, despite the Samaritan's low status and wickedness. But no: the first twist is that the priest and the temple assistant – both overtly religious and supposedly virtuous – walk past, presumably because they don't want to 'pollute' themselves. The second twist is that the Samaritan acts like a neighbour to a man who, in different circumstances, might have treated him harshly. And this from a man whom the expert in religious law would have regarded as the lowliest form of human being. The Samaritan overcomes prejudice against him in order to reach out to the injured man. The third twist is that the Samaritan doesn't just administer first aid, he also pays for the man's convalescence out of his own pocket. The lesson is clear: all are human, despite cultural, ethnic, and religious differences.

If a Samaritan can realize this and act on it, so can we. Jesus is inviting us to extend the empathy we naturally feel towards our immediate neighbours to all beings.

The woman caught in adultery

In another biblical episode, Jesus is teaching at the temple when some scribes and Pharisees (people with a keen interest in religious law) bring him a woman who has been caught in adultery.[19] They remind Jesus that, according to the laws of Moses, she must be stoned to death. The author of the gospel explains that these scribes and Pharisees want to bring an accusation against Jesus by trapping him. So they present him with a dilemma: if he passes judgement on the woman, they can accuse him of usurping the powers of a judge. If he lets her off, they can accuse him of flouting the law. It looks like they have him trapped.

They bring the woman before Jesus and ask him, 'What do you say?' Ignoring them, Jesus bends down and starts writing on the ground with his finger. Clearly, he needs time to think. When they continue to ask for a response, Jesus stands up and says: 'Let the person among you who is without sin be the first to throw a stone at her.'

Then he crouches down again and continues writing on the ground. There is a stunned silence in the crowd. One by one the scribes and the Pharisees leave, starting with the oldest. They realize that they have failed to trap him. In time, Jesus is left alone with the woman. He stands up and says, 'Dear lady, where are your accusers? Hasn't anyone condemned you?' She replies that no one has. Jesus says, 'I don't condemn you either. Go home, and from now on don't sin any more.'

With 'Let he who is without sin cast the first stone', Jesus invites the scribes and Pharisees to turn their attention from judging the woman to examining their own consciences. They realize that they are human and vulnerable. Perhaps they have done things that they regret. Sensing their own vulnerability in this area, they become more empathic towards the woman's position. None is willing to cast the first stone – to continue with their judging, blaming, and punishing. Perhaps they are able to see again the humanity of a person whom they have regarded as a sinner, and therefore less than human.

The word 'sinner' is an 'enemy image', concretizing judgement and blame. According to this way of thinking, the woman has sinned against the tribe and deserves punishment. By focusing the crowd's attention on their own consciences, Jesus breaks down this groupthink. It's *much* easier to cast the second stone – it gives a self-righteous relief and confirms membership of the group. However, Jesus asks each person to take responsibility as an individual, rather than a group member. When they bring their attention to what they have in common with the woman, and their own vulnerability, the enemy image breaks down and they can no longer act as an irresponsible group.

Is there a common thread running through the two parables? Perhaps it's the importance of recognizing our *common humanity* with people whom we regard as other, by race or religion. This recognition relies on first acknowledging our own pain and vulnerability. The two experiences are complementary.

Shelley's love, or imaginative identification

Let's come 1800 years closer to the present day, to the poet Shelley, who saw a link between morality, love, and the capacity to imagine:

> The great secret of morals is love; or a going out of our
> own nature, and an identification of ourselves with the
> beautiful which exists in thought, action, or person,
> not our own. A man, to be greatly good, must imagine
> intensely and comprehensively; he must put himself in
> the place of another and of many others; the pains and
> pleasures of his species must become his own.[20]

Putting oneself in the place of another amounts to the same thing as the *Dhammapada*'s 'making comparison of others with oneself'.[21] Shelley identifies the secret ingredient of morality as the faculty of imagination. By imagination he means the process of identifying with what is beautiful in others. Shelley saw this moral development as deeply challenging. The person who undertakes this path of the imagination must imagine 'intensely and comprehensively'. They must connect imaginatively with many others, so that the joy and suffering of their species becomes their own. Like the Buddha before him and others after him, Shelley sees a link between morality and the capacity to identify imaginatively with others' experience. In other words, ethics is based on empathy.

Coming back down to earth, we need to recognize that empathy takes practice. Here is another opportunity to train your empathy muscles by identifying imaginatively with someone else. What do you imagine is going on inside Jim as he gets held up in traffic and misses his train?

 Empathy exercise

- Purpose of this activity: to train your capacity to imagine the experience of others by seeing their feelings and needs
- Tools: a notepad or journal and a pencil
- Time: 5–10 minutes

For each of the sentences in italics, try to guess the feelings and needs behind Jim's words. If you want, you can compare your guesses with mine at the end. Bear in mind that there are no right answers.

'I was in my car, driving to the station. *I had to catch a train to go to a job interview.* The traffic slowed down and stopped. *I was sitting there, hands holding the wheel, wondering what was up ahead.* We moved a little bit, then stopped dead. Five minutes passed, then ten, then fifteen. *I started to get really worried about missing my train.* Eventually the traffic moved and I put my foot down to get to the station. *I parked the car, jumped out, and ran.* As I reached the platform, *the train was slowly moving away from me, with its doors closed. I stopped and panted and sweated. What should I do now?*'

I'll Meet You There

My guesses

I had to catch a train to go to an interview. Jim wants to be seen as reliable. He's also in touch with the needs behind the new job: security, possibly respect, meaning, creativity, and so on, depending on what the job means to him.

I was sitting there, hands on the wheel, wondering what was up ahead. Now he's getting tense, and needs ease and clarity about what's happening.

I started to get really worried about missing my train. He's feeling worried now, and needs ease and reliability. He wants to understand the impact of the current situation.

I parked the car, jumped out, and ran. He's probably feeling desperate by now.

The train was slowly moving away from me, with its doors closed. He has a sinking feeling of disappointment in his chest and stomach. He needs support and ease.

I stopped and panted and sweated. He's feeling exhausted and panicky. He needs space to catch his breath.

What should I do now? Jim is looking for clarity and creativity in how to deal with the situation.

To understand all is to forgive all.

– Evelyn Waugh[1]

Chapter three

·····································

The origins of the word 'empathy'

If we accept the theory of evolution of life on earth, the capacity for empathy has been around for at least 100 million years. However, the word 'empathy' didn't appear in the English language until the twentieth century. It was coined in 1903 to translate the German word *Einfühlung*. *Einfühlung* comes from *ein* 'in' + *Fühlung* 'feeling', and translates as 'feeling into' or 'feeling oneself into'. *Einfühlung* was originally coined in 1873 as a term of art appreciation by the German psychologist Robert Vischer.[2] It meant the way humans project their feelings onto or feel their way into a work of art such as a painting.

The German psychologist Theodor Lipps took up *Einfühlung* and broadened its use to feeling into the experience of another person as a way of understanding them. Later Lipps offered *empatheia* as its ancient Greek equivalent, from two words: *en* meaning 'in' or 'into' and *pathos* meaning 'feeling'.[3] English-speaking psychologists enthusiastically embraced this term and naturalized it into English as 'empathy'. Before 1903 there seem to have been a number of words used to describe what we now mean by empathy, including sympathy, love (as in the Shelley quotation in the previous chapter), and pity.[4]

A modern dictionary defines empathy as 'Identification with and understanding of another's situation, feelings, and motives.'[5] Identification is the emotional component of empathy: sensing what the other is feeling. Understanding is the cognitive aspect: clearly perceiving the other's situation, motives, and needs.

Imagine you're waiting at the checkout. You're not in a hurry, so you have a chance to listen to the woman in front who is pleading with her crying toddler. The toddler doesn't want to stay in his seat. The woman is trying to take her groceries from the trolley and put them on the belt. You can sense how she's feeling: frustrated, tense, perhaps annoyed and embarrassed. And you can understand her situation and her motives: she's in a tight spot, she wants to check out and get home without taking up too much of other people's time. On top of this, she wants to give her child attention. With all this going on, she needs ease and understanding for her situation, perhaps cooperation and support. Is this how you would read her situation?

Carl Rogers

Moving further into the twentieth century, we meet Carl Rogers, widely regarded as one of the founding fathers of psychotherapy research.[6] His seminal 1957 paper identified empathy between therapist and client as a vital factor in supporting the client's personal growth. The therapist tries to understand the client's thoughts and feelings from the client's own perspective, and tries to communicate this understanding to the client.[7]

Rogers went on to outline the implications of this theory for research, psychotherapy, and programmes aimed at personal growth. His theory became the model for various schools of humanistic psychology, including the client-centred and person-centred approaches. Rogers applied his findings on the benefits of empathy to education and work settings, then politics and peace work.

Later in life, Rogers enthusiastically approved this subtle, shifting definition of empathy:

> Qualitatively it is an active process of desiring to know
> the full, present and changing awareness of another
> person, of reaching out to receive his communication
> and meaning, and of translating his words and signs
> into experienced meaning that matches at least those
> aspects of his awareness that are most important to him
> at the moment. It is an experiencing of the consciousness
> 'behind' another's outward communication, but
> with continuous awareness that this consciousness is
> originating and proceeding in the other.[8]

Put simply, empathy is the process of reaching out to receive a person's meaning, whilst acknowledging that their experience is constantly changing.

Rogers loved to listen deeply. He found it created deep, life-enriching connections. He credited deep listening with everything he knew about individuals, about personality, about relationships. It put him in touch with what he regarded as being universally true. He saw how this process of deep listening supported personal growth and development. People looked grateful. They felt a sense of release. They wanted to tell him more about their world. They moved forward energetically with a newfound sense of freedom. They became more open to the process of change.[9]

And he absolutely loved being heard: 'I can testify that when you are in psychological distress and someone really hears you without passing judgement on you, without trying to take responsibility for you, without trying to mould you, it feels damn good!'

Marshall Rosenberg and Nonviolent Communication

The first time I saw Marshall Rosenberg was in London in 2002. I found myself in a crowd of about 400 people sitting facing a stage. I noticed several people talking by the side of the stage. One of them was a man who looked to be in his late sixties. He was dressed casually, even a bit scruffily. He had a peculiar hangdog expression. I hadn't yet seen a photo of him, so, if someone had said to me, 'Look, that's Marshall Rosenberg!', I would have said, 'No way!'

The man with the hangdog expression walked up the steps onto the stage, sat down, and started talking about how we communicate. Later in the evening he played the guitar and sang one of his songs. The words 'failed country-and-western singer' and 'I could do better than that' drifted through my mind! Despite this unpromising start, his words sank in.

He said that whatever we humans do, we are trying to fulfil our needs. Needs are the resources life requires to sustain itself. They include air, water, rest, and food, which support our physical well-being. They include needs such as understanding, support, honesty, meaning, and compassion, which support our psychological and spiritual well-being. With needs defined in this way, we can see that all humans have the same needs, regardless of gender, education, religious belief, or nationality. What differs from person to person is the strategy for fulfilling needs. Although it was new to me, this kind of understanding isn't new. Albert Einstein said a similar thing:

> Everything that the human race has done and thought
> is concerned with the satisfaction of deeply felt needs
> ... Feeling and longing are the motive force behind all
> human endeavor and human creation.[10]

Through Marshall, I began to get a glimpse of how I might enrich my life in ways that would also enrich the lives of others. Previously I'd held the rather black-and-white view that I could either serve myself (be selfish) or serve others (be unselfish). Perhaps this is quite a common view in our culture. Now I sensed the possibility that I could care for myself *and* care for others.

Later I made a link with the Buddhist tradition when I came across a passage in a Buddhist text that describes how a bodhisattva, the ideal Buddhist, assesses the needs of beings and then decides how to assist accordingly.[11] I started to get curious about Marshall and his background. In his childhood, he wondered why some people stayed compassionate while others used violence. As a young adult, he trained as a clinical psychologist, including a period of study with Carl Rogers. During the civil rights movement in the 1960s, he was involved in preparing communities for desegregation (changing institutions to bring white- and black-skinned people together again). He found that all the while people used labels such as 'black' or 'white', 'good' or 'bad', 'right' or 'wrong', they reinforced their separateness. In contrast, bringing people's attention to their feelings and needs helped them to understand each other and recognize their common humanity.

Over the next few decades, he developed a process that he came to call Nonviolent Communication, based on principles of honesty and empathy. The Centre for Nonviolent Communication (CNVC.org) was founded by his students and supporters to continue his work. Like Rogers, he extended his field from psychotherapy into education, work settings, and peace-building. He also investigated intimate relationships, parenting, social change, mediation, and conflict resolution. As Nonviolent Communication is the main context in which I've learned and practised empathy, we'll spend the next chapter exploring it more deeply.

Philosophers and mystics

The Jewish-German philosopher-mystic Martin Buber also explored the topic of empathy. Buber's intention was to bring about unity on every level: within the individual, between individuals, between nations, between humankind and the inanimate world, and between God and the universe.[12] Buber noticed that many people relate to the people around them as *objects* – as things that are separate from them. He also noticed that some people relate to those around them as *subjects* – being like them and connected to them. He pointed out that the second group of people are more in alignment with reality – we are always in *relationship* with the people and things around us. So we have a choice about how we relate to people and things. We can relate to them as an It or as a Thou. Relating as a Thou implies a sense of presence, mutuality, directness, familiarity, connectedness, and ineffability. This second way of relating implies the twin aspects of empathy: connection and imagination. In relationships, Buber recommended asking, 'Do you relate to another person in an I–It way or as an I–Thou?'

As a teenager, I found something similar in reggae. Reggae is a kind of blues-soul music, with lilting rhythms. The lyrics are often driven by Rastafarianism, a form of mystical liberation theology. Rastafarians tend to say 'I and I' when others would say 'we', as in 'I and I are going outside now.' I and I is a difficult phrase to draw out – it's more of a mood than a philosophical concept. I and I recognizes the total unity and identification of oneself with the other. There are not two persons here, but two

'I's. The word 'we' isn't strong enough to communicate this. I and I is an expression of the oneness and fundamental unity of two persons.[13] It is empathy on a mystical plane.

Modern psychological research: is empathy a motive for helping others?

In the 1970s, researchers at the University of Delaware created an 'emergency' situation to test the link between heart rate and helping behaviour. The researchers chose to measure heart rate as an indicator of empathic distress – feeling distress when we see another person's distress. Seventy-five female undergraduate students were wired up with electrodes and sat listening to a situation in another 'room'. In the other room (actually only a tape-recorded voice coming over the intercom), the victim stopped what she was doing in order to restack a pile of chairs that she described as threatening to topple over. A moment later there was the sound of falling chairs. The victim screamed that the chairs were falling on her; she screamed three times before a prolonged silence. Concealed video cameras recorded whether the bystander stood up or opened the door to go and help.

As might be expected, bystanders stood up or opened the door faster when they believed that they were the only witness to the emergency. However, what really excited the researchers was that the bystander's heart rate began to accelerate an average of 20 seconds *before* they got up from their chair to help the victim. And the faster the observer's heart rate accelerated, the quicker she got up to help. The researchers concluded that the empathic distress led to the subsequent helping behaviour.[14]

Scientific attempts have been made to establish empathy as a moral motive – a motive for acting ethically. Experiments show that people who witness someone in distress are liable to respond empathically or with helping. The witnesses feel distress – their heart rate goes up, their hands sweat – and this distress is relieved when they do something about the situation. The relief is experienced as a warm glow of satisfaction. Those who don't help remain distressed, and don't experience the warm glow.[15]

It's hard not to conclude that empathic distress is a motive for acting morally or compassionately. It could be argued that people help only because it gives them a warm glow, and not to alleviate the victim's distress. However, other research suggests that empathic helpers continue to feel distress if the victim's distress is not alleviated for some reason.[16] Despite the fact that helping gives people a warm glow, it does matter that the victim's distress is *actually* alleviated.

But what is the real connection between empathy and distress? In order to empathize with another's pain, you create a map in your own brain of their experience. However, you need to keep reminding yourself that *you* aren't actually in pain – it's the other person. Sympathizing, or feeling distress on behalf of the other person, actually gets in the way of genuine empathy and compassion. Blurring the distinction between self and other, so that everybody's suffering becomes your own, doesn't increase your capacity for empathy: it decreases it. People who maintain a clear distinction between self and other are more able to respond empathically than people who can't.[17] How can we put this into practice? By making a clear distinction between what *others* are feeling and needing and what *we* are feeling and needing.

Empathy and cruelty

Researchers have also explored the connection between lack of empathy and cruelty. Simon Baron-Cohen, director of the Autism Research Centre at the University of Cambridge, has been trying to understand human cruelty by replacing the term 'evil' with 'lack of empathy'.[18] He has looked at groups of people who appear to lack empathy – those diagnosed with borderline personality disorder, narcissism, or psychopathy. His argument is that violence of any sort can occur in empathy's absence. This seems an important insight, and can allow us to see people who are violent not as irredeemably 'bad', but as deficient in empathy.

In brain-scan studies, people who have been diagnosed as 'psychopathic' or 'borderline', on the autistic spectrum, or with

Asperger's syndrome have decreased functioning in the ten areas associated with empathy. This is what we would expect. However, we need to remember that human beings are not machines that can be broken or fixed. Human motivation is more subtle. The relation between areas of the brain, one the one hand, and consciousness and motivation on the other is much more complex.

People with a diagnosis of borderline or narcissistic personality, autism, or Asperger's syndrome tend to be *oblivious* to the pain their actions stimulate. They are not so much cruel as indifferent. The only real case of cruelty is people who have psychopathic tendencies. These people have the capacity to imagine another person's pain, but they don't feel any concern about it. They make a choice to extend their empathy or not. Their lack of concern for the welfare of others is due to a lack of motivation to care about others, rather than a lack of ability to do so.[19] They have a dim awareness of the pain that their actions stimulate. Dangerously, they are capable of feeling satisfaction from this pain. My guess is that this satisfaction derives from seeing pain reflected in another's eyes, because it gives them some understanding of and recognition for their own deeply veiled pain.

The capacity for empathy can be measured – it is distributed throughout the population. Some people have a lot of it, most people have some of it, and a few people have none. People with a lot of empathy might be good therapists. People with zero empathy are liable to treat others roughly or instrumentally, and are likely to be responsible for most of the human cruelty in the world. The remainder of the cruelty is likely to be committed by those of us who experience temporary lapses of empathy.

However, Baron-Cohen's central argument, that human cruelty appears to involve a lack of empathy, is not new, and does not provide a complete or satisfactory answer. And, in attempting to reclassify cruelty as a psychiatric disorder, he undermines the ethical principle that we choose our actions and are responsible for the likely consequences.

No research is complete without a gene study. Is there a gene for empathy? Nearly all of the studies on twins who share 100 per cent of their genes say yes, there is a hereditary component to empathy.[20] Other studies on the general population have revealed that there are a number of genes associated with empathy. These genetic factors interact with biological, environmental, and psychological factors in determining how empathic each individual is.

Oxytocin and bonding

Empathy has been linked to oxytocin – the love and bonding hormone. Oxytocin influences social and emotional behaviours. Its presence increases a sense of bonding, trust, and empathy, and decreases stress. Researchers have found a correlation between levels of oxytocin in a person and their ability to empathize. Some people seem to be genetically more empathic and less stressed than others. Stress itself seems to block the capacity for empathy. The more stressed you are, the less you are able to empathize with others.[21] This suggests a way to increase your ability to empathize by reducing chronic and occasional stress. Perhaps this is one of the ways in which practising mindfulness meditation increases empathy – because it decreases stress.

Women, men, and sex

Are women better than men at empathizing? Does empathy make for better sex? Recent research has highlighted that women and men tend to be similar in relation to most psychological characteristics. However, behavioural studies suggest that females often perform better in navigating the emotional landscape than males. For instance, females seem to be better at picking up non-verbal cues such as facial expressions. And in studies, women generally come out as more empathic than men.[22] It's not clear whether this is due to nature or nurture.

Men and women seem to have slightly different experiences of empathy. Women tend to rely more on 'feeling the feeling' of the other, whereas men tend to rely more on a cognitive process of taking the other's perspective, while disentangling their own feeling from that of the other.[23]

However, there are difficulties with this kind of research. Experimentally, it's very difficult to measure true empathy. It's much easier to measure when someone gets emotionally activated when confronted with angry or fearful faces, and infer that empathy is taking place. But simply feeling the feeling of the other person is not empathy. Empathy involves resonating with the other's feeling and sensing their deeper motivations, all the while remembering that it is the other person's experience, not our own. It's not clear whether men or women have an advantage in this. And of course there may be differences from culture to culture that we haven't yet learned.

Back on firmer ground, research supports a link between empathy and intimacy. Understanding another's emotional experience and being able to convey it accurately and compassionately often leads to a deepening sense of closeness.[24] After all, couples able to guess their partner's thoughts and feelings are more likely to engage in activities that increase intimacy. Overall, empathy has been identified as an important predictor of the survival and breakup of marriages.[25]

Empathy has been identified as an important component in sexual satisfaction. There appears to be a gender difference here too. A 2011 study looked at how sexual satisfaction in young men and women correlated with certain qualities: self-esteem, autonomy, and empathy. The study found that young women (aged 18–26) who have greater self-esteem, a sense of autonomy, and a capacity to empathize with others also experience greater sexual satisfaction in opposite-sex partnerships. The three qualities may support each other. The achievement of sexual enjoyment may boost young women's self-esteem and sense of autonomy. Equally, self-esteem and a sense of autonomy may be important to young women's sexual pleasure since they facilitate sexual communication and exploration.

For young men of a similar age, however, it is only the capacity to empathize with others (not self-esteem or sense of autonomy) that goes with greater sexual pleasure. Empathy is the ability to take another's perspective, to see things from their angle and understand and respond to their emotions. It's likely that young men who have the capacity to empathize with others are more responsive to their female partner's needs, and thus initiate a positive feedback cycle of sexual satisfaction.[26]

Sex within partnership is an aspect of intimacy, and needs some consideration, even protection, for it to flourish. To preserve this sense of intimacy, I asked my partner Gesine to help me write about our personal experience. We can see several ways in which the ability to empathize increases sexual satisfaction.

Firstly, empathy creates a sense of bonding and trust. Empathizing and being empathized with brings us closer to each other. I am aware of Gesine's inner world, and Gesine mine. There is a sense of heart connection: mutual care, understanding, and love. Within this increased sense of closeness and emotional safety, there is greater openness for us to 'feel' each other, a safe place for experimentation and letting the other know what we like. Secondly, empathy increases our overall sensitivity towards each other, so we do more of what the other likes and less of what they don't like. Thirdly, we empathically sense when the other is aroused, and this increases our own sense of enjoyment. Finally, empathy helps repair conflicts and disconnections when they occur and allows for a renewal of intimacy.

I'm looking forward to reading other studies on empathy and sex that include diverse sexual identities, orientations, and cultures.

Empathy, sympathy, and charity

What is the difference between empathy and sympathy or charity? Empathy is appreciating and valuing what is fundamental to the other person, their deeper motivations, their physical needs, their hopes and dreams. It involves imagining how the other person might feel in their situation and what is important to them. Sympathy describes a range of emotional responses, such as feeling sorry for the other person, and can be heard in, 'I know how you feel', 'I feel exactly the same way', or 'I hear your pain.'[27]

When we sympathize, we try to summon up the feeling that corresponds to what we imagine the other person is feeling. For instance, if you think your friend is feeling upset about their dog dying, you might say, 'I know how you feel.' This is likely to lead to distress for you, and actually hinder real empathy. When sympathy extends to charity, it implies that you are putting yourself above the person you are helping, treating them as a 'worthy cause'. The difference between empathy and sympathy/charity is summed up in a quotation from a 1970s aboriginal women's collective, 'If you have come here to help me then you are wasting your time, but if you have come because your liberation is bound up with mine then let us work together.'[28]

In his books and speeches, Barack Obama echoed this distinction between empathy and sympathy/charity. He saw empathy as the heart of his moral code, not simply a call to sympathy/charity, but something more demanding – a call to stand in somebody else's shoes and see through their eyes.[29] Obama tells a story of how he learned empathy from his time as a teenager living with his grandparents. His grandfather was warm-hearted, quick to anger, and easily hurt. The young Obama detested having to follow what he regarded as petty rules about borrowing his grandfather's car or rinsing things before throwing them out. They argued continually. With his developing skills as a lawyer, Obama found that he could usually win these arguments. But at some point these victories started to feel hollow, and he began to appreciate his grandfather's need to feel respected in his own home.

Later Obama came to see empathy as a fundamentally important quality, and echoed the view that it is the basis of social cohesion, social responsibility, social justice, and even resolving international disputes without war. So much war and conflict seem to depend on people's inability to recognize themselves in somebody else. However, Obama didn't pretend that developing empathy, a sense of our common humanity, is easy. It takes practice and effort. It's hard work to understand people who aren't like you, people who have different experiences and values. But, if you do the hard work, it turns

I'll Meet You There

out that people care about the same things, they have the same hopes and dreams. And ultimately, Obama says, that's what's going to be our salvation.

In the following culture clash you have a chance to start this hard work of understanding people who have different experiences and values. As you're reading, try to appreciate and value what is paramount to the two women, their deeper motivations, their physical needs, their hopes and dreams. Imagine what seems important to them.

 Empathy exercise

- Purpose of this activity: to see our common humanity by understanding what is important to others
- Tools: a notepad or journal and a pencil
- Time: 5–10 minutes

For each of the sentences in italics, try to guess what is important to the speaker. If you want, you can compare your guesses with mine at the end. Bear in mind that there are no right answers, and that empathizing is different from agreeing with either woman's world view.

Two young women are sitting in the student union at the University of North London. Chloe is from Essex, and Yasmin is an overseas student from Pakistan. They are talking about clothes.

Chloe: I don't know how you can wear that hijab [the scarf over Yasmin's head and shoulders]. *I mean, it's so demeaning, isn't it?*

Yasmin: *It's part of our religion.*

Chloe: *Yes, but you don't want to do everything that your parents tell you*, do you?

Yasmin: *I'm a good Muslim girl.*

Chloe: Come on, this is the twenty-first century. Women are strong now. *We can wear what we like.*

Yasmin: You don't know what it's like for us. *In order to survive, we need the respect of our family and neighbours.*

Chloe: Well, you're not going to get it like that round here. *People will think that you're backward, you're not civilized.*

Yasmin: *It's our way of saying that we are God's servant.*

Chloe: *It's like you're saying that you're someone else's property.*

Yasmin: *You don't understand our culture, our religion.* Don't put your ideas on us.

Chloe: *I just want you to be free!*

Make a note of your own guesses about what is important to each speaker. Then if you like compare them to my guesses below.

My guesses

I mean, it's so demeaning, isn't it? Chloe wants to understand Yasmin's clothes choices, and at the same time, self-respect is important to her.

It's part of our religion. Yasmin wants understanding for where the hijab came from, and respect for her religious beliefs.

Yes, but you don't want to do everything that your parents tell you. Chloe longs for freedom and independence.

I'm a good Muslim girl. Yasmin wants acknowledgement and respect.

We can wear what we like. Chloe wants the freedom to choose what she wears and the sense of empowerment that comes with that.

In order to survive, we need the respect of our family and neighbours. Yasmin needs to protect herself.

People will think that you're backward, you're not civilized. Chloe wants understanding for her perspective and her longing for freedom and empowerment.

It's our way of saying that we are God's servant. Yasmin wants understanding that her clothing is an expression of her longing for modesty and propriety, and reflects her place in the world.

It's like you're saying that you're someone else's property. Chloe wants autonomy, freedom, and dignity.

You don't understand our culture, our religion. Yasmin is desperate for understanding.

I just want you to be free! Chloe wants understanding for her intentions – she wants to contribute to freedom in the world

How did you get on? Make a note of it. Did you hear the judgements on the surface, or the underlying needs and values?

Part 2

Empathy and Nonviolent Communication (NVC)

Empathy is a respectful understanding of what others are experiencing.

– Marshall Rosenberg[1]

Chapter four

....

Marshall and the Palestinians

Despite my unpromising start with Marshall Rosenberg, I hung around long enough to learn that the NVC process has two aspects: honesty and empathy. Honesty was familiar to me, but empathy was new. Over the next couple of years, I came to realize that it was the missing ingredient in my emotional and spiritual life. It gave me the key to understanding clearly and precisely the workings of my own consciousness and the capacity to reach out to others, especially in difficult situations.

It's hard to assess the power of empathy unless you have seen it transform a dangerous situation. In the workshops I attended with Marshall, he was fond of telling the story of a visit to Dheisheh refugee camp in Bethlehem in the West Bank. He was there to present Nonviolent Communication to a mosque of about 170 Palestinian men. Being of Jewish-American origin, he was aware that he might not be received favourably. As he was speaking, a wave of commotion spread through the audience. Marshall's translator whispered, 'They are saying that you're American!' A man in the audience leaped to his feet and yelled as loudly as he could, 'Murderer!' A dozen voices joined him, 'Assassin!', 'Child-killer!'

Marshall had trained for this moment. He had practised hearing the feelings and needs behind hard-to-hear messages. So when he heard 'Murderer!' he didn't express himself by justifying or apologizing for his government's actions. Instead he chose to empathize, by keeping his attention on what the man in the audience was feeling and needing. He had learned that this was a more reliable way to create connection, especially in a heated situation.

Marshall had some clues about what the man was feeling and needing. On the way to the refugee camp, he had seen empty tear-gas canisters lying on the lawn outside. They had been shot into the camp the night before. Each canister had the words *Made in USA* clearly stamped on the side. He knew from this and other things that the refugees were deeply angry towards the USA for supplying tear gas and other weapons to Israel. He also reminded himself that it didn't matter whether his guess was accurate – what mattered was his sincere effort to connect with the man's humanity. This is what he said:

MBR: Are you angry because you would like my government to use its resources differently?

Man: Damn right I'm angry! Do you think we need tear gas? We need sewers, not tear gas! We need housing! We need our own country!

MBR (relieved that his first guess, anger, has landed, and that he now has extra information to work on): Are you furious because you'd like support to improve your living conditions and gain political independence?

Man: Do you know what it's like to live here for twenty-seven years with my family and children? Do you have the faintest idea what it's been like for us?

MBR (guessing that the man wants understanding): Sounds like you're feeling very desperate and hopeless that anyone can really understand what it's like to live under these conditions. Is that so?

Man: Do you have children? Do they go to school? My son is sick! He plays in a sewer! His classroom has no books!

MBR (acknowledging the pain behind the questions rather than answering them directly): I hear how painful it is to raise children here. You'd like me to know that what you want for your children is what all parents want – a good education, a healthy environment...

Man: That's right, the basics! Human rights – isn't that what you Americans call them? Why don't you all come here and see what kind of human rights you're bringing?

MBR (sensing the man's sense of injustice): Would you like more Americans to be aware of the depth of the suffering here, and be aware of the consequences of our government's actions?

The dialogue continued, with the man expressing his pain for nearly 20 more minutes. All the while, Marshall listened for the feeling and need behind each statement: he didn't agree or disagree. Once the man felt understood, he was open to hearing why Marshall was at the camp. An hour later, the man invited Marshall to his home for a Ramadan dinner. Marshall kept a warm connection with this man for many years, and fondly remembered being an honoured guest at the man's home whenever he was in the region.[2]

Rosenberg also organized a training retreat that brought together twenty Israelis and Palestinians. It was so difficult to set up that all the participants had to be flown out of the region to Switzerland to protect their safety. The workshop started with Marshall asking participants to pair up, take a walk, learn about each other, and come back to share their findings. Thus began several days of listening and connection across the divide, resulting in participants dropping their enemy images of each other and forming strong bonds that lasted beyond the workshop.

In one dialogue my dear friend Hagit Lifshitz, an Israeli-born NVC facilitator, supported Dorit, an Israeli woman, to empathize with Waseem, a Palestinian villager. The dialogue began with Waseem criticizing Dorit for not doing anything about the occupation: 'You see how terrible our situation is, then you go back home and do nothing!' Dorit blamed back: 'You Palestinians want us to do the impossible! We can't control the army and the government!'

Hagit, the facilitator, encouraged Dorit to focus on feeling and needs. What Dorit said next changed the course of the dialogue: 'I hear your pain and despair. I hear a deep wish of yours that I and my friends realize and imagine what many-sided suffering you go through every day. Is that it...?' Waseem replied, 'Na'am' ('Yes', in Arabic). He wished that Dorit could be with him to witness the suffering. He felt relieved and grateful to have been heard.

Later in the dialogue, a Palestinian man acknowledged Israelis' memories of horrors under the Nazis, and their fears when they heard Arabs saying things like, 'We'll throw them into the sea.' There was a silence in the room. The man went on to comment, 'I feel shame, when I remember this expression. I realize now that we, Arabs, express our own fears and tension when we say things like that. I wish we knew how to express our needs and feelings in a different way.'[3]

As a trainer following in Marshall's footsteps, I've been fortunate to witness moments of profound and healing connection as a result of empathy. In 2012 I was one of a team of trainers, along with Hagit Lifshitz, that led a nine-day healing and reconciliation event on the West Bank for about a hundred Israelis and Palestinians. We taught Nonviolent Communication in personal life and how to apply it to the larger context. Community dialogues touched depths of pain and fear on both sides. One small group session involved Ruthie, a woman of Jewish origin in her early thirties. She hadn't spoken much in the first few days. When it came to her turn to speak, everyone was curious to hear why she had come.

In a quiet, matter-of-fact voice she described how she'd been on a bus travelling from Tel Aviv to Jerusalem. It was late at night and the road was quiet. The windows were closed and all the passengers were asleep. Ruthie was shaken by a sudden movement. A voice cried in Arabic, 'Allahu Akbar'. There were screams. She saw a knife flashing above the head of the driver. The bus lurched sideways. Other passengers rushed to the front and dragged the attacker away from the driver. The driver, bleeding from his wounds, put his foot on the brake and brought the bus to a stop.

(As Ruthie spoke, I noticed that I had stopped breathing because of my own terror of sudden, violent death, and my deep longing for safety. Turning my attention to Ruthie, I guessed that beneath her words was the same longing to live in a safe world.)

I'll Meet You There

Ruthie continued: the attacker was still struggling, but the passengers had got the knife from him. They pushed and dragged him off the bus. Somebody checked the driver. Miraculously, his wounds weren't deep. A woman offered her scarf to bind them. Somebody else called the police. Ruthie and the other passengers assembled outside to look at the attacker. He was a well-dressed Arab of medium height, in his mid-twenties. In the light of the street lamp, he looked terrified.

'Kill him now, before the police get here. He would have killed all of us!'

'No, we will wait for the police to deal with him.'

(I felt relieved to hear that the man wasn't killed instantly – appreciating the humanity of the passengers' response. I also felt horror when I imagined what the police would do to him. I was puzzled what Ruthie might be feeling. I guessed that she might be in shock.)

Ruthie stood silently, shaking. Weeks passed. Ruthie felt a numbness creeping into her heart and mind. She came to believe that she had died that night. It was just her ghost that went to work and ate with her family and walked among the living. At times she felt anger towards 'the terrorists', at other times shock, even depression. But then the all-consuming numbness returned. Now Ruthie was here, telling her story to a group of Israelis and Palestinians who had come to listen to each other.

'There's no point in taking sides', she said, looking directly at the group. 'That man was a human, too. How will we bring an end to this? How are we going to find peace?'

Ruthie had told her story, delivered her message, and been heard. There was no need for us to reflect her meaning to confirm that we had heard and understood. It was clear enough. In that moment of silent empathy, Ruthie found the peace that she was longing for – the peace that comes from being heard and understood.

The Nonviolent Communication (NVC) process delivers empathy where it's needed. It isn't just for overt conflict: it has been found to be effective in a variety of other contexts. A study among men on parole in northern California suggested that the practice of NVC can boost empathy.[4] Other studies have found it supports openness in distance-learning mentoring relationships, increases well-being in hospital settings, promotes communication and collaboration skills, reduces violence and improves relations between staff and patients in psychiatric institutions, reduces conflict among teenage girls, reduces rates of reoffending among persistent offenders, and has supported long-term reconciliation efforts in war-torn areas such as Israel–Palestine, Serbia and Bosnia, and Sri Lanka.

In Brazil, with the help of a United Nations Development Programme grant, the Ministry of Justice hired NVC trainer Dominic Barter to develop a conferencing model and train facilitators for new restorative justice pilot projects. Barter called his process restorative circles. The programme serves large numbers of youth and has trained thousands in restorative principles and practice. The process Barter developed has since spread to other cities and countries.[5]

Feelings come from needs

What makes NVC so powerful is its unique clarity that our feelings come from our needs. In a conversation with one of his senior students, Rosenberg describes the moment when this occurred to him. He was asking himself what causes feelings. One day it hit him that feelings were really just talking about their underlying needs.[6] When people express their feelings, they're giving feedback about whether their needs are met or not. Once he understood this, other things became clear. We are responsible for our feelings, because they come from what's important to us – our needs. What other people do or say may be the stimulus for our feeling, but our feeling springs from the needs that are alive in us. It becomes easier to empathize with others, because they are also trying to meet their needs – needs that we have in common with them.

Imagine you're driving with passengers in the car when another driver pulls in in front of you. You brake suddenly in order to avoid hitting the back of the other car. Your passengers are jolted. After the initial shock of braking, you probably feel annoyed, even angry. Now, here's where NVC comes in. The other driver's actions are the stimulus or trigger for your feelings. But where do the feelings actually come from? The initial feeling of shock probably comes from a need for *safety* and *awareness*. You weren't expecting something like this to happen, so you need to update your expectations rapidly. Once you have taken care of safety and updated your expectations, the feelings of annoyance and anger probably come from needs for *ease* and *consideration* – for yourself and your passengers.

Clarifying feelings and needs empowers us. We're no longer the passive recipients of other people's actions. Nobody 'makes' us feel things. We have a choice about how we respond to what happens. That choice is within our power. We could choose to respond differently.

Viktor Frankl was a concentration camp survivor who wrote a celebrated book called *Man's Search for Meaning*. He sought to find meaning in the horror of his wartime experiences. He found it in a sense of choice about how he responded to what was going on around him. He brought his awareness into the space between stimulus and response. In that space, he argued, lies our power to choose, and in our power to respond lies our growth and our freedom.[7]

There are similar concepts in Buddhist psychology. The relationship between feelings and needs corresponds to the relationship between *vedanā* or 'feeling', and *cetanā* or 'volition'. Feelings and volitions are two of five kinds of mental activity that are always present in human consciousness.[8] Any particular *vedanā* can be pleasant, unpleasant, or neutral, and is said to be the result of previous volitions (*cetanā*). As products rather than causes, feelings don't influence our future states of consciousness. By contrast, volitions strongly influence our future states of consciousness. Rosenberg's concept of feelings and needs corresponds to this.

Let's go back to the emergency braking situation. Rosenberg would guess that you would be feeling shock, and that this comes from an underlying need for safety and awareness. Buddhist psychology would understand the situation in a similar way – your feeling of shock arises in dependence on volitions (longings) for safety and awareness. In both systems, feelings give feedback about what is going on inside the organism. Feelings are one of nature's natural feedback mechanisms, providing information about what is important for surviving and thriving.

The distinction between feelings and needs unravels a Gordian knot faced by writers on empathy. Some authorities say that empathy means feeling what the other person is feeling.[9] However, empathy is more complex than simply feeling the same as the other person. To understand empathy, it is necessary to look at the psychological processes underlying the relationship between what the two people are feeling.[10] What underlies a person's feelings? In some cases, thoughts seem to fuel people's feelings, but this doesn't seem to go deep enough. Common sense tells us that empathy involves understanding the deeper motivations or volitions that lead people to feel and act the way they do.

In his 1959 paper, Carl Rogers was clear that empathy was for both feelings and their deeper motivations. He described empathy as the process of sensing the hurt or pleasure of another person as they sense it, and perceiving the *causes* of those feelings as they perceive them.[11] There isn't just one word to describe these causes or deeper motivations. Some people like the word 'values', however there are drawbacks to this. Values can point to something that is too heady. Sometimes people say they value things when they are talking about a good idea, rather than something that they have fully integrated into their being. After years of searching for a suitable word, Rosenberg settled on 'needs' to indicate these deeper motivations.

Needs have an embodied, visceral quality. When people talk about their needs, they often touch their stomach or solar plexus. Their tone of voice and facial expression confirm that they really are in touch with the wellspring and inspiration of their lives. In some quarters needs have a bad press – they are regarded as selfish or egoistic. If we want to use the word, we will have to be clear that needs include spiritual needs such as freedom, wholeness, integration, beauty, meaning, understanding, and compassion, as well as psychological needs such as connection, mutuality, and honesty, and physical needs such as air, water, and food.

The big picture: the Tree of Compassionate Connection

Once I started sharing Nonviolent Communication, I looked for a way of showing the 'big picture' in a visual, symbolic form. The challenge was to show both the intention and learnable skills in one image. I found it in the Tree of Compassionate Connection, originally known as the NVC Tree of Life, as developed by NVC trainer Inbal Kashtan (see Figure 1).

Compassionate connection is the heartwood of this tree. This is the intention and purpose of Nonviolent Communication. Compassionate connection means relating in ways that lead to everyone's needs being valued and met. It is compassionate because it takes everybody's needs into account. It is connection because the tree focuses your attention on the quality of connection that will increase the welfare of all beings.

Down below the surface in the inner world are the roots of self-empathy and self-compassion. This is your connection to yourself, connecting with what's alive in your heart. It is also your connection to the earth, the roots that give the tree stability and resilience.

In the outer world the tree reaches upwards and outwards to connect with others. Broadly speaking, you can do this in two ways: empathy and self-expression. Both can be either verbal or non-verbal. Empathy is connecting with what's alive in the other person's heart. Self-expression is communicating what is alive in your heart to the other person. You can imagine these branches as arms reaching out to embrace the world.

There is a correlation between the roots and the branches. In a healthy tree, the crown is no greater than the roots. The biomass above the ground is no greater than the biomass below the ground. This reminds us of the importance of the roots. The extent to which you have grown the roots of self-empathy corresponds to the extent to which you can reach out to others through empathy and self-expression.

A few years ago I read a story in the newspaper about the Eden Project in Cornwall, UK. The project is home to the two largest greenhouses or 'biomes' in the world. Since 2001 these giant conservatories have housed various tropical and Mediterranean trees. In recent years a number of trees have fallen down, much to the surprise of the Eden Project's founders. Why was this? Surely these trees were some of the most protected in the world?

The founders called in some biologists to study the fallen trees. In the autopsy, they found that the trees had no roots to speak of! They went back to report their findings. The founders were astounded. Was it the soil? No. Was it the bedrock? No. Was it the humidity? No. Was it the micro-organisms and bacteria? No. They had thought of everything. But the fact remained that these trees had no roots to speak of. In the end they had to go back to basic mechanics to find the answer. There was no wind in the biomes! The trees had never felt any wind, so they didn't 'think' that they needed to develop roots. Finally, the trees had simply toppled over with their own massive weight. No wind, no roots!

It turns out that some wind is necessary for the resilience of an organism. Without it, a tree won't feel its roots challenged and put effort into developing deeper roots. Now I'm not saying that any amount of wind is a good thing. Clearly, a hurricane at any time of life may blow the tree over or distort its growing shape. However, if there's no wind, there will be no roots! Growers who grow large quantities of tree seedlings in greenhouses have got round this problem by setting a fan on the seedlings. They move the fan round the greenhouse so that the seedlings put out roots in all directions.

What does wind represent in human terms? Stress or challenge, often coming from other people. I'm not trying to glorify stress in a 'no pain, no gain' way. I'm just noticing, on reflection, a connection between wind and roots. In my own life I can say that some of my deepest roots have grown in response to some of my strongest challenges. I imagine that's true for all of us.

Marshall Rosenberg developed his empathy skills over many years through practice, reflection, and experience. In the following exercise, see if you can identify the feelings and needs behind this man's words. If it helps, imagine what might be important to him.

I'll Meet You There

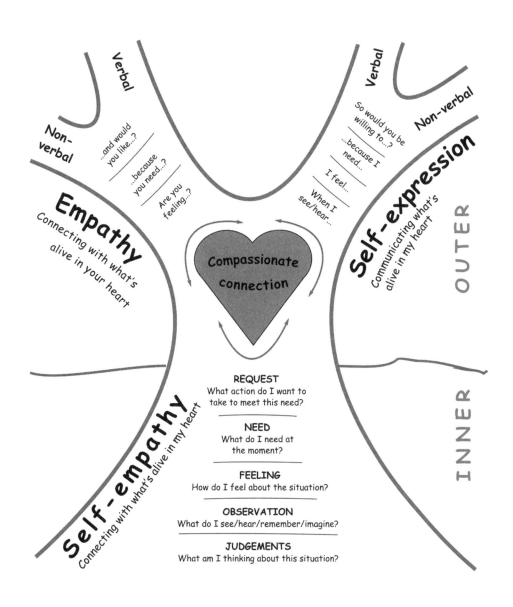

Fig. 1 The Tree of Compassionate Connection.

Empathy exercise

- Purpose of this activity: to identify the feelings and needs behind the words of the speaker
- Tools: a notepad or journal and a pencil
- Time: 5–10 minutes

For each of the sentences in italics, try to identify the speaker's feelings and needs. If you want, you can compare your guesses with mine at the end. As before, bear in mind that there are no right answers.

Tom is a man in his sixties from the UK. He wants to talk about the impact of retiring from his job.

'I didn't think that retirement would have such an effect on my life. *Of course I'm looking forward to having more time.* Now I can do whatever I want. *But what really hurts is not having something useful to do.* I miss the children and families I worked with. Now I just feel useless, like I'm hanging around, waiting for something. *People used to listen to what I had to say, they took me seriously.* I had a position that gave me influence and impact.

Of course I made a mistake just before I left. I missed a deadline to send out a recommendation for a child. It was one of my last cases. *That was embarrassing.* It was a shame that that had to happen just as I was leaving.

The work gave structure to my days. Now it's a choice between doing the washing up and watching the TV, and my wife tells me to do the washing up. There's no point any more. *I'm no longer important in the greater scheme of things.* I've lost my part in that. My work team still keep in contact, and ask for my opinion about certain cases. *It makes me feel that I still matter. At the same time, I really want to close that chapter and get on with the rest of my life.'*

I suggest you cover up my guesses below and make a note of your own guesses about Tom's feelings and needs. Then, if you like, compare them to my guesses.

My guesses

Of course I'm looking forward to having more time. I sense that Tom is enjoying his newfound freedom.

But what really hurts is not having something useful to do. However, he's feeling hurt because he's lost his primary means of contributing to life.

People used to listen to what I had to say, they took me seriously. He's lost a substantial amount of contact (connection) that he had at work, and the sense of being valued.

That was embarrassing. He's feeling guilty about missing the opportunity to contribute to the child's welfare, and embarrassed because he wants to keep his dignity and respect.

The work gave structure to my days. Tom is feeling sad about losing the structure that gave him predictability and ease in meeting his other needs.

I'm no longer important in the greater scheme of things. Tom is feeling sad and possibly hurt because he has lost a sense of being valued, of mattering and belonging.

It makes me feel that I still matter. At the same time, I really want to close that chapter and get on with the rest of my life. I sense that Tom is feeling genuinely torn, because he enjoys being valued but also wants a sense of completion and wholeness.

Instead of offering empathy, we often have a strong urge to give advice or reassurance and to explain our own position or feeling. Empathy, however, calls upon us to empty our mind and listen to others with our whole being.

– Marshall Rosenberg[1]

Chapter five

....

How not to empathize

Sometimes we say things that are supposed to be helpful and supportive, but aren't received that way. It's important to distinguish between empathy and its close neighbours, for instance pity and sympathy. As a study of doctors and patients found, 'Pity rarely helps, sympathy commonly helps, empathy always helps.'[2]

When we're learning a new topic, it can be easier to explore its opposite before clarifying what the topic itself actually is. It's the same with empathy – initially it's easier to grasp what it isn't than what it is. Here's how not to empathize.

> You've just returned to work after a minor health issue and you're telling a friend at the office about it. 'Have you tried Chinese herbs?' they ask. No, you haven't. 'It must be all those extra hours you've been putting in. I would've taken some of your case load, but I've been incredibly busy myself.' It could be, you say, you have been very busy. ... They reply, 'But you can't be that busy if you can afford to take time off for something as minor as this.' You go silent. Then they change tack and say, 'It could be worse. Last year you had that operation. At least this isn't going to lay you up.' No, that's true, you say. They launch into a story, 'Do you know, that reminds me how terrible last year was for me, health-wise. I must have been off work for at least six weeks in total.' You find yourself sympathizing with them, and lose connection with what you were saying. 'Anyway,' they say, 'you've got to keep your spirits up. There's no point in feeling depressed about it.' You half-heartedly agree with this. Then they start asking you for specifics, 'When did it start? Have you seen a doctor? Are you

eating properly?' You start wondering why you ever called this person a friend. Somehow they pick up on this, because they say, 'Oh yes, I know how you feel. I get low like that when I'm not feeling well.' When you tell them that you've been to see a doctor, but he said that there was nothing wrong with you, they say, 'Oh you poor thing! You didn't go and see *him* did you? He's so unsympathetic.' By this time, you just want to get back to your desk, but they continue in a cheerful tone, 'You may be sorted in other ways, but you're a bit of a loser when it comes to looking after yourself. Never mind, if you could only get the right attitude, this could turn into a real growth experience for you. I've got a book I could lend you about optimum health. I mean, it's been my bible, and I've had much worse stuff wrong with me.'

How does this story sound – painfully familiar? It illustrates a number of things that are unlikely to be received as empathy:

- giving advice/fixing it;
- explaining it away;
- correcting it;
- pitying;
- consoling;
- telling a story;
- saying 'don't feel...';
- sympathizing;
- colluding;
- investigating/interrogating;
- evaluating;
- educating;
- one-upmanship.[3]

Can you spot them in the dialogue above?

Fig. 2 How not to empathize.

Examples: 'Have you tried Chinese herbs?'; 'I've got a book I could lend you about optimum health.' Other examples: 'I think you should...'; 'If I were you...'; 'How come you didn't...?'

Giving advice/Fixing it

What's going on: In your enthusiasm to 'help', the desire to relieve your own discomfort, or a moment of unmindfulness, you lose awareness of the other person, forget about 'connection before correction', and 'empathy before education', and jump in with a solution.

It is unlikely to be received as empathy. Unless the person has been fully heard, it's unlikely that they are ready for advice/ suggestions. Inadvertently you are diverting the speaker's attention away from their own feelings and needs to focus on yours in offering the advice. By contrast, empathy keeps attention on the speaker.

Suggestion: Wait until the speaker has uncovered his/her deepest need and is feeling relieved, before offering advice. If you sense that you are at this point, you could say, 'I've got a suggestion – would you like to hear it?'

Explaining it away

Example: 'It must be all those extra hours you've been putting in. I would've taken some of your case load, but I've been incredibly busy myself.' Other examples: 'I can't do it, because...'; 'She only said that because you...'; 'But I didn't mean to...'.

What's going on: For balance, you're putting another person's point of view forward (which may also be yours). Inadvertently you're taking the attention away from the speaker to yourself and your motivations.

Correcting it

Example: 'But you can't be that busy if you can afford to take time off for something as minor as this.' Other examples: 'That's not how it happened'; 'You're the one who started...'; 'Excuse me... I never said that!'

What's going on: You want to get the story straight, so you try to correct the 'facts'. Even if your version is more accurate, the other person may not be ready to hear it.

Suggestion: Try empathizing first. As Marshall Rosenberg used to say, 'Empathy before education' and 'Connection before correction'.

Pitying

Example: 'Oh you poor thing!' Other examples: 'I feel so sorry for you!'; 'How can people do that?'; 'You don't deserve to be treated like that!'

What's going on: In your enthusiasm to help, you focus on the other person's pain and assume a position of being okay, competent, or resourceful in relation to them. You forget that you have the same needs as them. Pity distracts attention from the speaker to you. The speaker will probably pick up that you have put yourself above them in some way, with the assumption that you are okay and they aren't. This is unlikely to meet their need for dignity and respect, even if they are in genuine need of help.

Consoling

Example: 'It could be worse. Last year you had that operation. At least this isn't going to lay you up.' Other examples: 'It wasn't your fault...'; 'You did the best you could...'; 'There are plenty more fish in the sea.'

What's going on: In your enthusiasm to help, or fear of the speaker getting lost in their pain, you try to distract their attention from their unmet need to one of their needs that is met. When a person is talking about a painful situation, they primarily want understanding for what's important to them. Until they get this, they are unlikely to be able to hear a reminder about something that's 'going well'.

Example: 'Do you know, that reminds me how terrible last year was for me, health-wise. I must have been off work for at least six weeks in total.' Other examples: 'That reminds me of the time...'; 'Do you know, yesterday I was talking to...'.

Telling a story

What's going on: In an effort to distract the speaker from their pain, or let them know that they aren't alone, you tell a related story about yourself, usually with a moral to it! However, telling a story takes attention away from the speaker and what is alive for them. Connection before correction!

Example: 'You've got to keep your spirits up. There's no point in feeling depressed about it.' Other examples: 'Cheer up. Don't be sad'; 'Stop complaining!'

Saying 'don't feel...'

What's going on: Because of your discomfort with seeing someone else's pain, or a belief in 'positive thinking', you try to persuade the speaker to feel something different. Empathy is primarily for the speaker's deeper motivations. Feelings are feedback about these deeper motivations. Trying to change what a person is feeling is like trying to get them to replace a warning bulb on a car's dashboard. It has no effect on what's going on in the engine underneath, and may be misleading in future.

I'll Meet You There

Example: 'Oh yes, I know how you feel. I get low like that when I'm not feeling well.' Other examples: 'I feel exactly the same'; 'I feel your pain.'

Sympathizing

What's going on: You're trying to feel what the other person is feeling. You want to connect with the speaker, and you're trying to do this by identifying with them and bringing up the same feeling in you. In a subtle way, you've lost awareness of the person in front of you. Empathy is appreciating and valuing what is fundamental to the other person: their needs, their hopes and dreams. Sympathy inadvertently shifts the focus back to you. In addition, by attempting to match the feeling of the speaker, sympathy ignores the deeper level of motivation. Feelings give you feedback about this deeper level – they are not the level itself.

Trying to connect on the level of feelings is like skating on thin ice. It can be exhilarating, but you're liable to fall through the ice and get a cold shock of disconnection! Marshall Rosenberg was once asked about the relative importance of feelings and needs in empathizing. He said that feelings are 5–10 per cent of the connection, and needs the remaining 90–95 per cent. You may get lucky and make a connection on the basis of feelings. Sometimes you really do seem to be feeling exactly the same as the person you're with, for instance when you're in love with someone! However, you don't *really* know if the feeling you call love is the same as theirs. Besides, feelings come and go. You won't always be feeling the same as the person you're with. You're going to find life very difficult if you can only connect with someone when you're feeling the same as them.

Sympathy isn't just a weaker form of empathy, it can actually block empathy. In empathy, we are as present as possible to the other person's experience *without* feeling what they are feeling. Feeling what they are feeling can prevent us from experiencing the depth of empathic connection that is possible. For instance, feeling distress in response to another person's distress may lead you to pull away, reducing the likelihood of empathy and compassionate action.[4] An 'empathic distress' response actually impedes empathy.[5]

There's nothing 'wrong' with sympathy and empathic distress. Humans do these things to get connection. They often work, because the other person gets the intention behind them. However, sympathy and empathic distress are unlikely to create the same depth of connection and healing as empathic connection itself.

Suggestion: Do some self-empathy first. Try to find out what your needs are. Perhaps you're upset because you want the people you care for to be safe. Perhaps you want to contribute. When you're more connected to your own needs, turn your attention back to the other person and acknowledge what is important to them.

Example: 'You didn't go and see *him* did you? He's so unsympathetic.' Other examples: 'Tell me about it!'; 'How true! I agree with you'; 'Isn't that always the way?'

Colluding

I'll Meet You There

What's going on: You identify with the speaker and agree with their point of view. Colluding often goes with sympathizing. You'd think that people would like being agreed with. Isn't that what everybody wants? Sometimes when people offer sympathy they are simply agreeing with the other person. Obviously, this agreement appears to create connection. However, genuine empathy doesn't imply agreement. Empathizing and agreeing are two separate things. In empathy you are connecting with the needs that are alive for that person, not agreeing with their world view or the strategies they are using to meet their needs. That's not to say that you never offer your point of view. When you have heard a person out, they are usually keen to hear your response. It's only then that you reveal what's in your heart, when you are confident that the other person's ears are open. Reminder: empathizing is different from agreeing.

Example: 'When did it start? Have you seen a doctor? Are you eating properly?' Other examples: 'What made you do that?'; 'Why didn't you call?'

Investigating/Interrogating

What's going on: In your rush to make a connection, you lose mindfulness that asking questions to get a better understanding for yourself might be distracting for the speaker and make it more difficult for them to stay with their experience. Investigating and interrogating distract the speaker's attention from what's really important to them, their feelings and needs, to what you see as the 'facts' of the situation.

Example: 'You may be sorted in other ways, but you're a bit of a loser when it comes to looking after yourself.' Other examples: 'You're being unrealistic'; 'Your problem is that...'; 'If you weren't so defensive...'.

Evaluating/Diagnosing

What's going on: Evaluating and diagnosing distract attention from the speaker to *your* need, to be heard and understood. A diagnosis of the speaker's psychology is likely to be heard as blame and criticism. If it is, the speaker may find it difficult to stay connected with the painful feelings that arise. Empathic sensing invites the speaker to check in with their feelings and needs, respecting that they are the authority in their inner world. In this way, it supports the speaker's dignity.

Example: 'Never mind, if you could only get the right attitude, this could turn into a real growth experience for you.' Other examples: 'What is this telling you?'; 'You could learn something from this'; 'This could turn into a very positive experience for you'; 'Everything happens for a reason!'

Educating

What's going on: In your enthusiasm to teach the speaker 'a lesson' (i.e. meet *your* needs for learning and contribution), you lose sight of the fact that the speaker may need empathy before education. However, from the speaker's point of view, it's probably a distraction. Once the speaker has been fully heard, they will naturally be curious about what they might learn from the experience. At that point, your reflections on what could be learned may be invaluable. Again: empathy before education.

Example: 'I've had much worse stuff wrong with me.' Other examples: 'That's nothing...'; 'Listen to what happened to me!'

One-upmanship

What's going on: You want to put things into perspective. What the other person is going through isn't such a big deal. You lose awareness of the other person and focus on your need for perspective. One-upmanship distracts the speaker from their feelings and needs. Through repeated experiences, I can say that comparing two sufferings doesn't lessen either of them. In addition, it may not meet the speaker's need for respect, dignity, and self-esteem. The speaker may hear it as, 'Your pain doesn't matter, because it's less than mine (or someone else's).'

If you remember what it is like to be on the receiving end of advice, story-telling, sympathy, pity, educating, and so on, you may be less likely to employ them yourself. In the following exercise, try to recall when someone spoke to you in these unempathic ways, and the impact it had on you. Then try to imagine what the person could have said that you would have received as empathy.

Exercise: things that are unlikely to be received as empathy

- Purpose of this activity: to reflect on your own experience of things that are unlikely to be received as empathy, and imagine what you would have received as empathy
- Tools: somewhere to sit quietly and comfortably, and a notepad or journal and a pencil (optional)
- Time: 10 minutes

Recall a conversation in which someone spoke to you in some of the ways explored in this chapter:

- giving advice/fixing it;
- explaining it away;
- correcting it;
- pitying;
- consoling;
- telling a story;
- saying 'don't feel...';
- sympathizing;
- colluding;
- investigating/interrogating;
- evaluating;
- educating;
- one-upmanship.

For instance, when someone was determined to give you advice, and all you wanted was to be heard. How did you feel at the time? Relaxed? Or tight, frustrated, disappointed, and hurt?

How do you feel now, as you remember? What needs of yours are alive ... respect and consideration, understanding, or maybe just to be fully heard?

What would you have received as empathy? What pain did you need understanding and acknowledgement for?

After 5 minutes, review the exercise. What touched you? What did you learn? You might like to journal this.

Our ability to offer empathy can allow us to stay vulnerable, defuse potential violence, hear the word no without taking it as rejection, revive a lifeless conversation, and even hear the feelings and needs expressed through silence.

– Marshall Rosenberg[1]

Chapter six

....

Intention, presence, and focus

People often hear what is being said to them as judgements, whether expressed verbally or not. Imagine someone close to you saying, 'You never listen!' Does this statement increase the likelihood that you will listen and cooperate? According to Rosenberg, this kind of criticism is a tragic expression of feelings and unmet needs. It's tragic because it decreases trust, connection, and the likelihood that we will get our needs met. Once we understand this, we have the choice to hear every message as an expression of the person's present feelings and needs. Instead of reacting to the message and taking it personally, you might ask them, 'Do you want my full attention right now?' This gesture of empathy is the hallmark of Rumi's field, out beyond ideas of wrongdoing and rightdoing, mentioned in the Introduction.

The previous chapter looked at things that are unlikely to be received as empathy. The next two chapters explore the practical skills of empathy: intention, presence, focus, timing, and sustaining empathy.[2]

Intention

If you want to empathize, the first thing to ask is, why? It may seem obvious, but this is a very important question. What is your intention in empathizing? If your empathizing comes out of guilt, fear, or anger, it's very unlikely to be received by the other person as empathy. They are much more likely to receive your guilt, fear, or anger. If you are feeling these emotions, try spending some time reconnecting with yourself, either silently in self-empathy or by asking another person to listen empathically. When you have reconnected with your own feelings and needs, curiosity will naturally arise about what is important to the other person.

Contrary to popular understanding, empathy is not about meeting the *other* person's needs. The only person who has the power to meet their needs is them. Empathizing is a way to meet your *own* need – for connection. So we're not empathizing for the other person's benefit. If you are telling yourself that empathizing is a 'good thing to do' or that you 'should' empathize, your efforts to empathize are likely to come across as patronizing. In reality, we empathize for our own benefit: to meet our own need for connection and perhaps to contribute to life. This kind of honesty frees us up to stay connected with ourselves at all times.

But how to do this? You could begin by focusing on your intention to connect compassionately. If you have a spiritual teacher or guide, you could bring them to mind here. You could bring to mind the Buddha's vision of humans as lotuses in different stages of development. All humans began life somewhere. All are growing. All are in different stages of development. All are trying to fulfil their life potential. You could remind yourself that empathy is the aspect of compassion that meets people *where they are*, and not where you would like them to be.

Try formulating your intention. Marshall Rosenberg's was 'Creating a quality of connection that leads to everyone's needs being met through compassionate giving'. I like to say to myself, 'Going for connection, hanging loose to the outcome' or 'Let's see if we can get everybody's needs met.' Remember that it's not possible to meet your needs at the expense of another person's. Nobody's needs get met unless everybody's needs get met.

Don't get caught up in 'doing it right' – it's your intention that counts. Even if you do this in silence it will have an effect. Remember that you have a choice about how you meet your need for compassionate connection. You could just as easily choose to express yourself honestly or to stay in self-empathy (self-compassion) until you are ready to hear the other person.

To summarize: focus on your intention to connect compassionately, with an awareness that you have various choices as to how to act on it.

Presence

Empathy is not about doing something to somebody – it's a quality of presence. Marshall Rosenberg was once asked for a definition of empathy. Instead of giving an intellectual answer, he talked about empathy as full presence.[3] Presence can seem a mysterious word, but in this context he meant the kinaesthetic or embodied aspect of being with another person. Empathy is full presence to what is alive in a person at this moment. It brings in nothing from the past. The more you know about a person, the harder it is to empathize with them. The more you have studied psychology and are able to diagnose people, the harder it will be. You can bring in no thinking from the past. Marshall suggested that, if you know how to surf, you'll have more of a feel for empathy, because you will know in your body what it is about. Just liking surfing, empathy is about being present and 'getting with' the energy that is coming through you in the present. It is not a mental understanding.

Empathy is an intuitive body-sense rather than an intellectual understanding of other people's psychology. Marshall quotes the Chinese philosopher Zhuangzi, who claimed that true empathy requires listening with the whole being:

> The hearing that is only in the ears is one thing. The hearing of the understanding is another. But the hearing of the spirit is not limited to any one faculty, to the ear, or to the mind. Hence it demands the emptiness of all the faculties. And when the faculties are empty, then the whole being listens. There is then a direct grasp of what is right there before you that can never be heard with the ear or understood with the mind.[4]

This hearing of the spirit is full presence.

It's easy to slip into the idea that when you are listening you are 'giving' empathy. However, this is misleading. We don't *give* empathy. What we give is our attention, our compassionate presence. Sometimes the other person has the experience of 'feeling felt', of being understood and empathized with, sometimes not. Our presence, even our silent attention, can be a precious gift.

This presence has the quality of *following* rather than leading. Imagine you're reading a great book, and you're so absorbed in the story that you lose a sense of *you* reading it. There's just this great story happening. That's the quality of empathy.[5] How do you get to experience this? For most people, going out and learning to surf isn't practical, so we need something that you can try at home. You could invite someone around you to join you in trying the following exercise.

Exercise: leading and following

- Purpose of this activity: to get clear on the different qualities of leading and following
- Tools: another person to work with, space to move around, music to provide a pleasant soundtrack to the exercise (optional)
- Time: 10 minutes

Invite a family member or friend to do this exercise with you. Make sure that there is space around you to move freely. Remove any hazards such as things on the floor that you might trip over.

Stand facing each other. Decide who will lead first (you'll both get a go). Whoever is leading holds one hand out in front of them with the palm down. The person who is following lightly rests the fingertips of one hand on the back of the leader's hand.

The leader then moves their hand around as they wish. If you're the follower, try to keep light, consistent contact with your fingertips on the back of the leader's hand. You're not pushing the leader's hand, leading them. At the same time, you're not following so far back that you lose contact. You may find that thoughts about what just happened or anticipating what will come next get in the way, so just let your thoughts go quiet, and put your attention in your fingertips. You may find this easier if you close your eyes.

When you are both feeling confident, the leader can begin to walk and turn, leading the follower around the room. Remember that the leader is responsible for making sure that the follower doesn't bump into anything!

After 3–4 minutes, swap roles, so that you experience both leading and following.

After another 3–4 minutes, stop and stand opposite each other to review the exercise. What was it like to lead? What was it like to follow? People say that following gives them a direct bodily experience of being sensitive to the movement of another person. This is listening with the body, and is central to empathic listening. By contrast, leading is more like speaking.

To summarize: empathy is like surfing; you learn it with all your senses. It's not an intellectual understanding, but listening with your whole being. We don't *give* empathy; we give our attention, our presence. Sometimes this is received as empathy and understanding, sometimes not. Empathy has the quality of following, listening with the body, rather than leading.

Focus

In empathy you put your full attention on what is alive in the other person right now. You don't focus on what happened in the past, including your past judgements of them. You don't focus on the future – it hasn't happened yet! Connection and healing take place only in the present.

But what is meant by *what is alive*? What do you actually give your attention to? There are a number of ways to describe this, including taking the other person's perspective, standing in their shoes, seeing things through their eyes, and exploring what's deeply important to them. All these are helpful guides, however now we need to be more specific.

Try focusing on the person's feelings and needs. Feelings are feedback about whether needs are met or not. Needs are resources required to sustain life. Our physical well-being depends on our needs for air, water, rest, and food being met. Our psychological and spiritual well-being increases when our needs for understanding, support, honesty, and meaning are fulfilled. As already mentioned, all humans have the same needs. What differs is our strategies for fulfilling them.

According to the Chilean economist Manfred Max-Neef and his colleagues from the economic school of human-scale development, there is a list of fundamental human needs.[6] These are regarded as finite and classifiable, in contrast with wants, which are infinite. These fundamental human needs are common to all humans across time and culture. They are:

- subsistence;
- protection;
- affection;
- understanding;
- participation;
- leisure;
- creation;
- identity;
- freedom.

With the possibility that a tenth, 'transcendence', may in time become a universal need.[7]

Appendix A (see p.183) expands this list of nine basic needs for everyday use. However, be warned: looking down a list might actually make it more difficult for you to stay with your inner process. Rather than going by the list, see if you can find the words that describe what you are longing for, or what would give you more life.[8]

There's another problem with making a list of needs. When some people see it, they immediately think of Abraham Maslow's hierarchy of needs.[9] Maslow proposed that the need for self-actualization (realizing your potential) is the final need. This need manifests when lower-level physical and psychological needs have been satisfied. I'm just not sure about this. Is there really a hierarchy of needs? The relationship between needs seems more dynamic than hierarchical. Needs move through us moment by moment. Needs are life energy in motion. To borrow a phrase from Khalil Gibran's poetic masterpiece *The Prophet*, they are 'Life's longing for itself'.[10]

There is also evidence from sociology against a hierarchy of needs. Studies have been done with starving people, some of whom may care intensely about freedom and autonomy or meaning and purpose. They will sometimes put dignity or meaning above their hunger. The evidence for this is the existence of freedom fighters or guerrillas in some poverty-stricken areas.

Some people prefer to talk about values rather than needs. In practice there are a variety of ways to point to these deeper motivations (see the next chapter on *timing* for more suggestions). However, as mentioned in Chapter 4, 'values' does not fit as well as 'needs' as the default word for describing them. When people talk about their values, it can come across as quite heady. This feels different from when they are in touch with their deeper motivations.

By contrast, the word 'need' has an embodied, visceral quality. I've lost count of the number of times I've seen people touch or point to their stomach or solar plexus when they are talking about their needs. At the same time, I've noticed that their tone of voice, gaze, and posture are congruent in a way that tells me that the person really is integrating the wellspring and inspiration of their lives.

Occasionally I've heard a concern that the language of needs encourages people to become dependent on others. I can understand that this concern arises from the longing for personal responsibility and empowerment. I share this longing. However, in my experience the language of needs can be deeply empowering and supportive of efforts to take responsibility for the likely consequences of one's actions. Your feelings come from your needs. Nobody makes you feel anything. This is radical responsibility. To free things up further, you have a choice whether to meet your needs internally or externally. Ultimately you are the only one with the responsibility and power to meet your needs. And of course one of your options is to seek the support of people around you to help you meet them.

For many of us, our culture and upbringing hasn't made it easy for us to identify and accept our needs. Try the following exercise to become more familiar and comfortable with your needs.

Exercise: getting familiar with your needs

- Purpose of this activity: to make experiential connections with needs
- Tools: somewhere to sit quietly and comfortably, and a notepad or journal and a pencil
- Time: 10 minutes

Read through the needs diagram in Appendix A, taking time to savour each word and its associations. Imagine a situation when each need was met. Do you notice a different quality in your body for each need? Even a different location? What feelings or images arise as you silently connect with each need?

When you're ready, ask yourself if there are any needs on this list that you haven't been in touch with at some point in your life. Give yourself time to respond.

After a few minutes, ask yourself if you think that there is anybody in the building you are in who hasn't been in touch with these needs at some point in their life. Again, give yourself time to respond.

After a few minutes, reach out in your imagination to the people in the local town, the country, the continent, the entire world, and ask the same question: do you imagine that there is a human being who hasn't been in touch with all of these at some point in their life? Give yourself time to respond.

Review the list. Is this the list of universal human needs? Would you add or take away any? How do you feel? What is important to you right now? Make a note of it.

In empathy, you don't speak at all. You speak with the eyes. You speak with your body. If you say any words at all, it's because you are not sure you are with the person. So you may say some words. But the words are not empathy. Empathy is when the other person feels the connection with what's alive in you.

– Marshall Rosenberg[1]

Chapter seven

....

Timing and sustaining empathy

The moment of empathy is always silent. You might use words later to check if you're in touch with the speaker, or when you imagine that they would like a sign that you're really with them. Staying silent or using words is a choice. However, if you want to use words, you need to develop your skills to make it an active choice.

Let's say you've been listening silently to another person. When the speaker pauses, check you've heard what's important to them: 'Are you hoping...?' or 'Were you wanting...?' Ask a question rather than make a statement, because questions are more easily heard as respectful invitations. Once you've started empathizing with someone, you may be surprised how deep it goes. As explored in Chapter 5, it helps if you can hold back from offering solutions or helping the person to formulate next steps, at least until you're sure that they have had the opportunity to express themselves fully. Marshall used to say, 'Empathy before education' and 'Connection before correction.' If you jump in too quickly with solutions, the other person may get the impression that you're not really interested in *them*; you're only interested in fixing their problem.

Sustaining empathy

The initial message that you hear is usually just the tip of the iceberg. If you stay attentive, riding the wave of someone's feelings and needs, they will usually go deeper. Allow the speaker the opportunity to fully explore and express their inner world. When the other person has been fully heard, they will tend to relax and to go silent. You will probably notice a corresponding relaxation of tension in your own body. If you aren't sure whether the other person has fully expressed themselves, you can check before offering suggestions, corrections, and so on, by asking, 'Is there anything more you would like to say?'

One of my earliest attempts to sustain empathy was when I was working on the wards at Fulbourn psychiatric hospital near Cambridge in the UK. At the time, I was training to be an NVC trainer. From time to time I did a shift on the secure ward, where there were locked doors, fences, and specific times for activities during the day. One day, while I was looking at a newspaper, I noticed a man in his early twenties walking backwards and forwards in front of me. I recognized him as Eric, a guy I'd hung out with on visit the previous week. Only now his face seemed to be somehow twisted and he was saying, 'I'm not sick! It's the drugs that are making me sick. I've got a degree to finish. Why won't they let me go back and finish?'

There was loud music playing in the common area, but I could hear Eric's voice above it, and so, I guess, could everyone else. He was clenching his fists and looking from side to side. He looked very different from how I remembered him, when we'd chatted and walked outside in the garden. Eric was in the secure ward because his family and the doctors were afraid for his safety and the safety of the people around him. The doctors had diagnosed him with schizophrenia.

My immediate response to seeing Eric in this state was to feel sad. The week before I'd enjoyed connecting with him. Now he didn't even look at me as he walked past me, shouting, gesticulating, and clenching his fists. I doubted I could reach him. Perhaps he saw this in my face, because this time he faced me and spoke loudly and passionately, 'It's the drugs that are making me sick. I've got a degree to finish.'

Just a few days before, I'd been on a Nonviolent Communication course, learning how to empathize. Now, here was my chance. I decided to take the plunge and try it for real. In a voice that could be heard throughout the common area I asked, 'Are you pissed off because you want to get on with your life?'

'Yes!' he said, louder than before. 'And the f***ers are holding me down and injecting the drugs into my bum!'

If I had been quick enough, I could have asked, 'Do you want to be in control of your life?' But the moment had passed. Eric went back to walking up and down, repeating that staff held him down and injected drugs into his backside.

I felt disappointed. There had been a moment of connection, but then I'd lost it. After a while I went back to reading the newspaper. To my surprise, over the next five minutes Eric slowed down walking, talking, and gesturing. His voice became quieter, and eventually he came and stood in front of me again; 'You know,' he said, loud enough for everybody in the room to hear, 'we need more people like you in here ... people who understand what's going on.'

Now I felt elated, that I'd been able to keep a connection with him, even when those around me would have said that he was in a 'psychotic' state. So what did I do differently? Firstly, I didn't sympathize with him. I didn't say, 'I'd be angry if I was in your situation.' And I didn't try to console him: 'You'll pull through.' I didn't ask questions for the sake of my own clarity: 'How do the drugs make you feel?' As we saw in Chapter 5, these kinds of questions are unlikely to create connection.

Secondly, I didn't try to put my side of things, even though this was very tempting. I didn't say, 'If you carry on like that, the other nurses are going to jump on you and forcibly inject you.' I guessed that Eric didn't have the space to hear this. He probably would have got even angrier.

Thirdly, I tried to guess what Eric was feeling and needing. I did this because I wanted to keep my connection with him. I really missed our human connection. So I guessed that he was angry because he wanted the freedom to live his life the way he wanted. So that's what I asked him: 'Are you pissed off because you want to get on with your life?' I chose to say it this way because I thought it would be easier to hear than, 'Are you feeling angry because you need freedom?' In hindsight, I could also have guessed that he needed understanding ... that in his eyes he wasn't sick, it was the drugs that were making him sick.

I'm still delighted with how I kept my connection with him on that day. It helped me to realize the healing power of empathy.

Taking 'time in'

If we find ourselves unable to take in what the other person is saying, it's usually because we are in too much pain ourselves. As Marshall put it, 'We need empathy to give empathy.'[2] Try recalling the safety briefing on an aircraft. Part of it usually goes like this: 'Adults travelling with young children, please secure your own mask first.'

I vividly remember the first time I understood this. I was with my partner, also a certified NVC trainer. She was troubled how sometimes she found it deeply challenging to connect with the people around her. She wondered if it was to do with how connected she was to herself. I asked, 'Do you mean that if you're connected to yourself, it's easier to connect to the people around you?' She got really excited and said, 'Yes, that's it! That's it! I'm only half-way through my life, and already I know the secret!'

If you're finding it difficult to empathize, you could acknowledge this to the other person. You could tell them that you find it difficult to listen because of your own pain. They might respond by offering *you* empathy. However, sometimes you might choose to take 'time in' and give yourself emergency first-aid empathy. You can listen to yourself with the same quality of compassionate presence that you offer to others. 'Time in' is like time out, only it's a moment to connect to your inner world.

The former United Nations secretary general Dag Hammarskjöld once said, 'The more faithfully you listen to the voice within you, the better you will hear what is sounding outside. Only he who listens can speak.'[3] Awareness of others depends on your ability to listen to your inner voice.

In taking 'time in', you stop and become mindful of your breathing. You reconnect with what is important to you, what you feel and what you need right now. At first, it might seem that this process will take too long, and take you out of the exchange with the other person. If you become skilled at it, you can reconnect with yourself and resolve to return your attention to the other person. It can be very useful in a crisis.

I'll Meet You There

Here's a time when it worked for me: my partner (the same one as above) asked me to listen to her. She wanted to tell me about some things that I'd been doing that she was angry about. I found myself struggling to listen to her. When I spoke, I noticed that my voice had a hard, unfamiliar edge to it. When I heard the sound of my voice, I realized that I was feeling angry. I also realized that, if I spoke from my anger, we would lose the trust and connection between us. I had started out listening, and I wanted to honour this, so I managed to say, 'Could we come back to this?' She paused for several seconds, and said, 'Okay.' I went for a walk. On the walk I took time in and gave myself emergency first-aid empathy. Afterwards, I was ready to reconnect with her. I told her that I doubted I could hear her feelings (I was afraid that they would trigger my anger again), but I was hopeful that I could hear her needs. She paused for a moment, then said, 'My need is dignity. I need dignity.' I was touched that I could really hear her need. I felt the dignity in it. And I was totally relieved that I didn't hear blame or judgement of me. Both of us said that we felt sore about what had happened. However, we both still trusted in the other's intention to stay connected. Within 15 minutes we had re-established warmth and closeness.

Do you remember Eric? Here is the exercise that I did on the NVC workshop, a few days before my second encounter with him. It's a gentle reminder that we have a choice about how we listen to others. By doing this exercise repeatedly, you create and strengthen the pathways in your brain that allow you to respond compassionately in any situation. I recommend that you write down your responses to the questions. Writing things down seems to strengthen intentions and provides an opportunity for reflection afterwards.

Exercise: four ways of listening

- Purpose of this activity: to develop an awareness that there are different ways of listening to a challenging message; in particular, that you have a choice whether to hear blame and criticism, or unmet needs
- Tools: somewhere to sit quietly and comfortably, and a notepad or journal and a pencil (optional)
- Time: 15 minutes

Recall a painful message. Something you've heard said to you, for instance, 'You're always late' or 'You're selfish.'

Write down what you would say (or think) if you chose to judge and blame the person who gave you this message. This might sound like, 'Who are you calling late? How many times have you been late this week?' or 'You self-righteous bastard!'

Secondly, write down what you would say (or think) if you chose to judge and blame yourself. This might sound like, 'She's right. I'm always late for our meetings.' Or 'Yes, I'm so selfish.'

Thirdly, write down what you would say (or think) if you chose to hear the message in terms of what is alive in you. What feelings and needs are touched in you when you hear this message? It might sound something like this: 'I'm feeling, well, disappointed, because I'd like acknowledgement of the effort I made to get here.' Or 'I'm feeling sad, because I want to take everybody into account.'

Fourthly, write down what you would say (or think) if you chose to hear the message in terms of what is alive in the other person. It might sound something like this: 'Are you irritated because you'd like respect for your time?' Or 'Are you frustrated because you want everyone's needs to be taken into account?'

Remember, it's just a guess, and it's the intention that counts in creating connection. If your guess turns out not to be accurate, the other person will tell you what's really going on: 'No, it's not that. We don't see each other as often as I'd like. When you're late, we spend less time together.' Or, 'No, I want to know that there is space for me in this relationship.'

Review the exercise:

- Which was more familiar – blaming the speaker or blaming yourself? (One of these is usually our default.)
- What was difficult?
- What touched you?
- What did you learn?

I suspect that the most basic and powerful way to connect to another person is to listen. Just listen. Perhaps the most important thing we ever give each other is our attention... A loving silence often has far more power to heal and to connect than the most well-intentioned words.

– Rachel Naomi Remen, MD[1]

Chapter eight

....

Empathy archery

Since I've been learning how to empathize, I have often got it 'wrong'. What I mean is that the person I was listening to has told me, either by a shake of the head or by a 'No', that my empathy guess hasn't landed. I've had the sense of firing arrows towards a distant target, and most of them falling short or going wide. At these moments, I've felt discouraged and unhopeful of mastering the skills of empathy. However, I've just kept at it. I must have made thousands of empathy guesses, possibly even hundreds of thousands. By learning from the feedback, I've gradually got more accurate.

When I started supporting others to develop their empathy skills, I wondered how they would deal with these inevitable setbacks. I noticed that they seemed to have the same responses: sometimes they blamed themselves for 'being useless', and did the emotional equivalent of giving up and going home. And sometimes they did what I coached them to do – take a moment of self-empathy, then pick themselves up to empathize again.

To improve my skills as a coach, I tried to notice what I was actually doing when I was empathizing. From Marshall I'd learned to put my attention on the speaker's feelings and needs. However, most of the time I wasn't specifically focusing on them; I was getting a fuzzier, more general sense of what was going on for the speaker.

So I drew a target with two rings – 'needs' and 'feelings' – and started to think how I could expand it to include this fuzzier focus. I added two outer rings, which I called 'sensing what's important' and 'summarizing'. To my relief, empathizing got easier. I found I could relax my attention to include these other aspects of empathy, whilst keeping feelings and needs at the centre. In the end I added a further ring, 'listening in silence'.

This ring clarifies that words are very much secondary, and reminds us that most of the time we're silently sensing rather than searching for words (see Figure 3).

Empathy archery enlarges the target. If you're just aiming at connecting with feelings and needs, you might find that you struggle to hit the target at all. By enlarging the target to include sensing what's important, summarizing, and listening in silence, you make it more likely that you will be hitting the target more of the time.

The arrows came later. I was in Pune, India, facilitating an 'advanced' NVC weekend. I showed the participants my empathy-archery target, without the arrows, and said that I wanted some way of representing the empathy 'guesses'. I needed something to show a question, a sensing, coming from the heart. I explained that we frame our empathy guesses as questions, as enquiries, with a question mark at the end. This kind of enquiry is easier to receive as empathy than statements or diagnoses, which are likely to be heard as blame or criticism. Secondly, I wanted a heart shape, because empathy guesses are coming from the heart rather than the head. A heart can also show that I am reaching out in empathy as a way of meeting my need for connection.

Over lunchtime, one of the participants drew various different designs in her exercise book. In the afternoon we sat round and discussed their relative merits. In the end we chose the design you can see on the diagram, with an elongated question mark as the tip of the arrow, and the heart as its feather. The arrows are shown landing in all rings of the target, to emphasize that all the rings 'work', that is, they are likely to be received as empathy.

Listening in silence

Listening in silence is the outer circle of the target and the largest surface area, because this is what you'll be doing most of the time when you're listening. For most people, it's the easiest skill to develop. However, there are a few people for whom listening in silence is the most difficult part of the process – I apologize

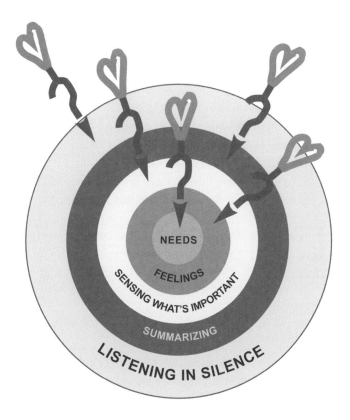

Fig. 3 Empathy archery diagram.

if that's you! Listening in silence is empathy *as presence*, just giving your attention to the speaker. If you want somewhere to put your attention, sense what is going on in the speaker's heart. Do this without words – leave them till later.

Rosie is a woman in her late twenties living in Bristol. She's been living with builders:

> In the apartment that I live in, there are lots of holes in the roof. They have constructed loads of scaffolding, and it's right above my roof. It's quite annoying... I can hear workers' feet banging as they walk over my roof. It feels a bit invasive – people trampling above my head all day. And they have the radio on all the time, so I've got these pop songs blasting through my head.

I give massage, and sometimes clients come to my house, and suddenly there's loads of drilling noise above our heads during the massage. It was really difficult to do the massage. I just couldn't get in touch with myself.

I haven't talked to the builders about it. I'm a bit shy of talking to them, because they're doing a positive thing in mending the holes in the roof. I actually had a leak in my roof, and the rainwater was coming down into my room. And anyway, I don't have much choice in the matter, as I don't own the apartment. But it is awful.

I listened in silence, taking in Rosie's words, tone of voice, posture, and gaze. I gave her my silent presence. Could you imagine doing this?

Exercise: listening in silence

- Purpose of this activity: to practise empathy as presence
- Tools: another person, a notepad or journal, and a pencil
- Time: 5 minutes

Ask a family member, practice buddy, or friend if they are willing to talk about something that is moderately uncomfortable for them for 3 minutes. Listen in silence. Give your attention. This is empathy as presence. If words come up, hold on to them until after the exercise. Notice anything else that comes up for you as you listen. Make a note of it at the time or at the end of the exercise.

How did you get on? Did you notice yourself nodding or saying 'Mmm ... mmm'? Did you keep eye contact, or look away? It is okay to nod – just notice what you're doing and what effect it has on the speaker. Some families and cultures like nodding – they appreciate it as a sign of paying attention. In other families and cultures they wonder what's wrong with you... Why are you nodding the whole time? The same with eye contact and going, 'Mmm ... mmm'. Notice what you're doing, and try to gauge its effect. Does the speaker seem to want more eye contact, or less? What happens if you look away for a while? Does the speaker seem to want to draw you back into eye contact? If so, increase eye contact to a comfortable level again.

Did you feel the urge to ask for more information? Perhaps you wanted to understand more fully, and give yourself time to tune in? I recommend that you resist the urge and just remain silent. Rather than asking for additional information, use the information you've already got: what they've said (or not said), their tone of voice, body language, and so on. If you ask for additional information, it's likely to distract them from what they really want to say.

Give the speaker the luxury of exploring what they want to say *at their own pace*. Allow them to bathe in the glory of knowing that they don't have to rush their words for fear of interruption. Allow them to expand into the silence. When there is a silent gap, after some time, something else might come up. This never happens in 'normal' conversations – there's no space for it.

Summarizing

Some people find summarizing a bit 'clunky'. They say that trying to remember what's been said takes them out of their heart into their head. There's some truth to this. However, most of the mediation processes I've come across rely on the skill of summarizing, so it has its place on the target. Simply wait for the speaker to pause or take a breath, and say back what you've heard, and check with the speaker, 'Is that it?' Keep the summary brief, so that the attention stays with the speaker.

I summarized Rosie's account in this way: 'You've got builders on the roof and it's really annoying. You haven't talked to them as the roof really needs mending. Is that it?' Rosie agreed. It was enough to confirm that I'd got the main points, and allowed her to continue with her story.

 Exercise: summarizing

- Purpose of this activity: to practise summarizing as a way of empathizing quickly
- Tools: another person, a notepad or journal, and a pencil
- Time: 5 minutes

Ask a family member, practice buddy, or friend to tell you about some moderate difficulty they are facing. If they're not willing, ask them to read

Rosie's account out loud to you. When the speaker pauses, summarize what you've heard in one or two sentences, and check with the speaker if it's accurate. After the exercise, in your review, ask the speaker what worked and what didn't. Make a note of it.

Summarizing is especially useful for listening to people who are speaking in an 'angry' way to you. If you confirm what you've heard them say, it can very quickly take the heat out of the situation. People want to be heard, and summarizing is one way of letting them know this.

Beware of going straight for the needs. It can feel hollow and empty, as if the listener is closing down the conversation too quickly. We all want to be heard, want to be met. Slowly move in towards the centre of the target. It's all about pacing, going at the speed of the speaker. Empathy is about *following*, not leading them anywhere.

Sensing what's important

When the other person pauses in their speaking, you could help them to clarify what's most important to them by using these openings: 'Is it important to you that...?'; 'Seems as if you wish...?'; 'Were you wanting...?'; 'Are you hoping...?'; 'Would you have liked...?'

Sensing what's important is between summarizing and sensing feelings and needs. It's closer to the heart, because it's tuning in to the significance of the words, rather than the literal content. However, it's more general than feelings and needs; it can include thoughts, requests, hopes, and wishes.

When Rosie paused for a moment, I asked, 'Is it important to you to have control in your personal space?' She said, 'Yes, it is', and I could see her shoulders drop with relaxation. Later I asked, 'Seems as if you wish you'd been asked first?' and 'Were you wanting respect for your personal space?' She nodded. I could have asked, 'Are you hoping they'll be finished soon?' or 'Would you have liked the landlord to talk with the builders about keeping the noise down?' Any of these were likely to be received as empathy.

Exercise: sensing what's important

- Purpose of this activity: to tune in to the emotional significance of what's being said
- Tools: another person, a notepad or journal, and a pencil
- Time: 5 minutes

Ask a family member, practice buddy, or friend to tell you about some moderate difficulty they are facing. When the speaker pauses, sense what's important to them using one of these openings:

- Is it important to you that...?
- Seems as if you wish...?
- Were you wanting...?
- Are you hoping...?
- Would you have liked...?

After the exercise, in your review, ask the speaker what they received as empathy and what they didn't. Make a note of it.

Some people find sensing what's important particularly liberating. They are no longer tied to feelings and needs. Asking 'Is it important to you...?' or one of the other openings helps them to relax and tune in to their natural intuitions. For others, this ring of the target is puzzling. It's not feelings and needs, and it's not summarizing, so what is it? Keep exploring what's in between.

Sensing feelings and needs

Moving closer to the centre of the target, there is another way of sensing that is more subtle and likely to take you deeper more quickly. It involves sensing what the other person is feeling *and* the need behind it. It takes more practice and skill than simply guessing what's important to them. However, it's worth the effort in terms of deeper connections, understanding, and healing.

In order to be able to guess what a person is feeling, you need to be able to distinguish feelings from thoughts. Here are some examples of feelings: hopeless, sad, or happy. Here are some examples of thoughts: 'I've been betrayed'; 'I'm useless.' These are evaluations or interpretations rather than sensation-like feelings. There's a list of feelings in Appendix B (see p.185).

In order to guess a person's needs effectively, you need to be able to distinguish needs from strategies. Examples of needs are connection, honesty, peace of mind, protection, and freedom. Examples of strategies are talking to my son this evening, buying a car, asking my friends round to dinner. There's a list of needs in Appendix A (see p.183).

The basic way is to ask, 'Are you feeling x because you need y?' I sensed Rosie's feelings and needs: 'Are you feeling annoyed because you'd like respect and consideration, that this is your home?' She replied, 'Yes, that's it', and went silent.

Could you imagine guessing another person's feelings and needs in this way? Remember that their feelings will give you feedback about what they need. If you aren't sure how they will respond, you can check it out with them first: 'I'd like to try something new while I'm listening this time. Are you okay with that? Tell me if it gets in the way.'

If you get lost, you can recall your intention to connect compassionately and bear in mind that there's no such thing as a 'wrong' guess. It is the reaching out for connection that is important and that is received as empathy. If your guess isn't accurate, the other person will let you know and correct it.

 Exercise: sensing feelings and needs

- Purpose of this activity: to practise sensing both a feeling and the underlying need
- Tools: another person, a notepad or journal, and a pencil
- Time: 5 minutes

Ask a family member, practice buddy, or friend to tell you about some moderate difficulty they are facing. When the speaker pauses, sense a feeling and a need, using this phrase: 'Are you feeling x because you need y?'

When you get more confident in sensing for both a feeling and a need, try varying the words:

- Are you feeling x because you really value y?
- Are you feeling x because you love y or because you would love y?
- Are you feeling x because you thrive on y?
- Are you feeling x because it's really important to you to have y?
- Are you feeling x because you really enjoy y or because you really appreciate y?
- Are you feeling x because you long for y?
- Are you feeling x because y really matters to you?
- Are you feeling x because you wish y?
- Are you feeling x because you would have liked y?
- Are you feeling x because you dream of y?

After the exercise, in your review, ask the speaker what they received as empathy and what not. Did you need to self-empathize as you went along? If so, make a note of your feelings and needs.

How did you get on? Was it easy to guess a feeling, but difficult to find the related need? If you guess a feeling, don't just leave it hanging there, give it a 'home' in a need. Empathy is a magic key that unlocks understanding and connection. It has some very delicate levers that key into feelings, and some others that key into the needs. Usually you need both kinds of levers to unlock the sense of really being heard and understood. The feelings tell you about how the need is being held. It's not just the content of the need that is important. The feelings tell you about *how* that need is being experienced at the moment.

Of course in real life, outside of a practice context, you'll use the whole target. Don't go mechanically through the rings, starting with listening in silence, until you hit the bull's eye. Instead, try bouncing your way towards the centre of the target, dropping back to an outer circle when you need to. Needs are still in the middle, because it's on the level of needs that we are most likely to connect. However, all of the rings work, and they are all part of the enlarged target.

If you're aiming at the needs and keep missing, the target reminds you to relax and spread out a bit. Perhaps just listen in silence for a while. Then have another go at using words. Beware of offering the speaker multiple feelings and needs – it can get confusing for them. How many times have you been asked a question and not had time to respond? If you ask a question, give the person a chance to respond.

What do you do when you hit the bull's eye of an accurate need? Do you just keep naming it? Take a breath. The target is actually like a spiral; if you touch a need on the surface, then the speaker will spiral down to a deeper need. If you touch that deeper need, then they will spiral down even deeper. Keep going, and the connection will get deeper.

How do you know when to stop? Go silent and see if something else comes up. If nothing else comes up, or if the other person gets up and leaves, then you know that they have received enough empathy for the time being. As mentioned in Chapter 7, when I was doing my NVC training I used to work in a psychiatric hospital. There are plenty of opportunities to empathize on the wards. If you miss one, another comes along a minute later. And that's just the staff!

My job was to talk to the 'patients', though by that time I was aware of the undermining effect of such labels. Often I would just go into the lounge and sit down next to someone. After a while, we'd get into a bit of a discussion, and on the basis of this I would try a couple of empathy guesses. Sometimes they would just get up and leave, without saying a word! I remember thinking, 'Oh no, I've missed the connection again! I'm a total loser; I'll never get it – I'm a waste of time.' Later I realized that they only got up and left when they had actually received empathy. If they didn't receive my words as empathy, they stayed seated. Perhaps it's something you could explore for yourself with the people you come into contact with.

Did you find that you were concerned that the speaker wouldn't be satisfied unless they found a solution to their problem? Look at your own experience. When someone else effectively guides you to identify your needs, you have trust that you can work out a plan of action for yourself. Empathy clears away the driftwood that's in the way of your own intuition about what you need to do. Empathy is empowering – it galvanizes your own resources. When you're listening, you can trust that the speaker also has this capability, rather than filling the space for them. Concentrate on creating connection and understanding. Once connection and understanding have been established, if necessary you can offer yourself as an extra resource for problem-solving.

Use the whole target. If you go straight for the feelings and needs, the speaker might feel that it's too abrupt. Listen in silence for a while to help them (and you!) warm up. Coming back to what we said at the beginning, the bigger the target, the more likely you are to hit it. Don't give yourself a hard time. Make it easier for yourself: enlarge the target.

Part 3

A Buddhist perspective

Could a greater miracle take place than for us to look through each other's eyes for an instant?

– Henry David Thoreau[1]

Chapter nine

···

Empathy and mindfulness

Empathy and mindfulness are an unlikely pair, given that mindfulness seems to be to do with attention and awareness, whereas empathy is more emotional. But research suggests that, if you increase your mindfulness, you also increase your empathy.[2]

In one striking study, participants were divided into three groups. One group received mindfulness tuition consisting of spoken instructions and a poem. Participants were encouraged to be aware of, and accepting towards, whatever thoughts and feelings arose. 'There is no need to try to control the breathing in any way ... simply letting the breath breathe itself ... as best you can ... also bringing this attitude of allowing to the rest of your experience.' The second group received positive-thinking instruction encouraging them to evaluate and attempt to control their thoughts and feelings. 'Noticing that you can have control over your breathing ... also bringing this strength and control to the rest of your experience ... trying to achieve a state of positivity and calmness...' The third group were encouraged to relax by listening to the sound of waves. All three groups then watched an emotionally evocative film clip and were asked to write about their reactions.

The mindfulness group wrote more about *other people*, including those in the film clip, than participants in the positive-thinking group. By writing about others, rather than themselves, they showed a greater capacity for empathy than the positive thinkers. Other research suggests that by writing more about themselves, the positive thinkers may actually have *increased* the likelihood of anxiety and depression. The relaxation group came in between these two and wasn't significantly different from either.[3]

···

Mindfulness is paying attention on purpose, and is the opposite of unmindfulness or distraction. The word 'mindfulness' contains the word 'mind'. This might suggest something that is primarily cognitive or even intellectual. However, this is misleading. In the ancient Indian languages of Sanskrit and Pali, the word for 'mind' and 'heart' is the same – *citta* (pronounced 'chitta'). So when we hear the word 'mindfulness', we need inwardly to hear the word 'heartfulness'. When we're mindful, we aren't imprisoned by shoulds or judgements about what ought to happen. Instead we experience each moment as new and fresh, with curiosity, openness, acceptance, and love.[4]

Gautama the Buddha was the prime example of someone living mindfully. We can imagine him sitting upright under the bodhi tree, legs crossed, a sense of peace radiating from his features. As we get to know him, we encounter other images, for instance his daily alms round. Holding his begging bowl with both hands in front of him, he walks from door to door, silently. But perhaps most resonant is that people who met him described him as having the 'elephant look'. This means that, when the Buddha speaks or listens, he turns his head fully towards you, with the majestic presence of an elephant. He's not glancing at the door or checking his phone while he's talking to you. He gives you his full attention.[5]

By contrast, here's an everyday story of unmindfulness from my own experience: I'm working from home today. I put some rice on for lunch and go upstairs to check my emails. One of the emails contains a link to a humorous video. I click on the link. While I'm watching it, my mobile phone rings, and I answer. It's a friend who wants support. Ten minutes later, as I finish the call, I glance at my computer screen and realize that I haven't checked all the emails. As I get to grips with one of the more difficult ones, I gradually notice an unpleasant burning smell in my nostrils. It's the rice! I stop what I'm doing and race downstairs to the kitchen. Smoke is coming from the rice saucepan on the cooker. I pull it off the stove, burning my fingers in the process. When I check later, the rice has stuck to the bottom of the saucepan in a black crust. All the rice tastes of smoke, and I decide that it's inedible. As I remorsefully throw it in the compost bin, I realize that I still haven't finished checking my emails, or started work 'properly'.

Does this seem familiar? Mindfulness is a key term in the Buddhist tradition, where it is said to have three aspects: (i) recollection and bare attention, (ii) clear comprehension and continuity of purpose, and (iii) ethical vigilance. Recollection and bare attention (*sati*) is a slippery term. Literally it means 'recollection, memory, calling to mind'.

In the Mindfulness of Breathing (*ānāpānasati*) meditation practice, you notice (*sati*) the physical sensations of breathing in and breathing out (*ānāpāna*). This is easy to describe and difficult to do. What happens? Instead of staying with the breathing, your mind starts to think about what you're having for your next meal, or something interesting that somebody said yesterday. The actual practice is noticing when your mind has drifted off, and bringing your attention back to the breath. That's the force of the 're-' in recollecting – bringing your mind *back* to the object of awareness.

Clear comprehension and continuity of purpose (*sampajañña*) is another slippery term – it can mean both. You recollect the past (*sati*) in order to predict and set goals for the future. Clear comprehension and continuity of purpose is the faculty that enables you to set your goal and monitor your progress towards it. It allows you to maintain mindfulness in and through time. Imagine you're riding a bicycle along the road. Recollection and bare awareness is your moment-by-moment conscious ability to pay attention to your sense of balance, and avoid falling off. Clear comprehension and continuity of purpose is your ability to bear in mind where you have come from, where you want to go, how to pedal, shift your weight, and turn the handlebars to get you there.

The third aspect of mindfulness is ethical vigilance (*appamāda*). This may seem surprising – what has mindfulness got to do with ethics? However, in the Buddhist tradition, mindfulness always has an ethical context. Ethical vigilance means being vigilant against 'unskilful' mental states that may harm yourself and others.[6] It means asking yourself ethical questions such as: 'What are the likely consequences of this action? How would you feel if someone did this to you? Do you wish to punish, or are you coming from a place of kindness and compassion? How could you support everybody's welfare here?'

The Buddha regarded mindfulness as essential to spiritual development. He said that it was the direct path for ethical purity, for overcoming pain and grief, and for realizing the freedom of Enlightenment. To give you some idea of its importance, on his deathbed, the Buddha's last words of encouragement to his disciples were, 'All things are impermanent. With mindfulness (*appamāda*) strive on.'[7]

The foundations of mindfulness are surprisingly down to earth: body, feelings, states of mind, and mental contents. Examples of mindfulness of the body are feeling the sensations of your breathing or your posture, whether walking, standing, sitting, or lying down. Examples of mindfulness of feelings are when you sense your feelings as pleasant or unpleasant. With the state of mind you sense the general condition of your consciousness. And with mental contents you notice the definite contents or objects of consciousness at any given moment.[8]

The Buddha didn't give a definition of mindfulness. He just said that it can be applied in these four everyday areas of experience. But he gives it a twist by encouraging people to practise mindfulness internally, externally, *and* both internally and externally. You can be mindful of *other people's* bodies, feelings, states of mind, and thoughts, just as much as your own.

This instruction could be taken as a sign of the thoroughness and completeness of the Buddha's teaching. By temperament some people prefer paying attention internally: to their own sensations, feelings, and so on. Conversely, some people prefer paying attention externally: to other people. The psychologist C.G. Jung characterized the former as 'introverts' and the latter as 'extroverts'. The Buddha encourages his disciples to develop mindfulness internally and externally to support balance and integration. In addition, sometimes it's easier to be 'objective' about what's going on in another person than in oneself, and vice versa. Attending 'both internally and externally' seems to imply practising mindfulness in the realm of interaction and communication.[9] The surprising implication is that empathy is an external aspect of mindfulness. Empathy is a mindful awareness of others and how we communicate with them.

Mindfulness also regulates and balances functions to support integration. According to the fourth-century Buddhist commentator Buddhaghosa, it protects the mind from lapsing into agitation or idleness.[10] Modern scientific research confirms this. Mindfulness encourages you to maintain your attention in the current moment, and experience thoughts and feelings as *passing through*, rather than as the totality of who you are.[11]

Have you ever felt swept along by the apparently unstoppable momentum of your own thoughts and feelings? Einstein was famous for his thought experiments, which expanded the field of physics. Let's try an Einstein-like thought experiment here. You're sitting in the dark of a cinema, watching a film. On the screen, the movements of the actors appear to be continuous. But this is a special screening. The movements of the actors gradually slow down, becoming jerky, until you start to see the individual frames of the film. In this frame, the male lead is raising a glass to his lips. A few frames later, he's drinking. A few frames later, he's smiling.

After a while of watching like this, you come to appreciate that what once seemed like a continuous, unstoppable stream is in fact made up of a series of discrete frames. In the same way, when you give greater awareness to your own mental states, you begin to be aware of the choices you are making, moment by moment. And as you make connections between your choices and their consequences, you start to experience a greater sense of freedom about what you might choose in the future.

Mindfulness appears to bring about a kind of internal attunement, by linking your current experience with your intention. Brain-scan studies have thrown light on what happens in the brains of meditators. The areas of the brain responsible for creating maps of other people's intentions are also involved in a kind of internal attunement.

The two are intimately connected: creating a map of other minds and an image of your own mental processes appears to use the same areas of the brain. It's well known that mindfulness meditation has a range of benefits, including support for the immune system, increased flexibility and balance in approaching difficulties, and increased well-being. What is less well known is that it improves relationships, through increasing our capacity for self-compassion and empathizing with others.[12]

How does this work? The answer seems to lie in special brain cells known as *mirror neurones*. One famous neuroscientist predicted that mirror neurones will do for psychology what DNA did for biology.[13] Initially these special cells were discovered in macaque monkeys. They fulfil functions that were thought to be performed by two separate areas of the brain: the motor system (responsible for movement) and the perceptual system (responsible for perceiving the world).

Mirror neurones fire when monkeys *perform* certain tasks. But, and here's the surprising part, they also fire when the monkeys *watch someone else* perform the same task. They appear to hold a representation of a particular action, whether the monkey performs the action itself or sees someone else doing it.

The original research was done in Italy.[14] The researchers found that a particular neurone fired in a monkey's brain each time the monkey grasped an object. This neurone was situated in a part of the monkey's brain known as F5, an area associated with motor activity (movement). However, the researchers were very confused to see that sometimes the neurone fired even when the monkey was just sitting quietly doing nothing. Then they noticed that one of the researchers had gone out and brought back an ice cream. Each time the researcher raised his arm to take a lick of the ice cream, they were shocked to see that the same neurone fired, with no 'motor' action on the part of the monkey at all.[15]

When the researchers came to name these new neurones, they drew on their understanding of mirrors. Mirrors give a first-person perspective ('I'm standing here, looking in this mirror') and a third-person perspective ('That's me, that's what I look like from the outside'). Because of their dual role in first-person (I grasp) and third-person (he grasps) perspectives, the researchers named them 'mirror neurones'.

Similar brain areas, that are active when both performing and observing an action, have been found in humans. This provides

I'll Meet You There

experimental evidence for the suggestion that the human brain creates maps of others' minds. We create a map of experience that we can refer to whether it's us performing an action or someone else. This allows us to engage in 'monkey see, monkey do'.[16] Through creating a map of another person's actions and intentions, we also tend to map their associated feelings.[17] These maps are probably underpinned by mirror neurones.[18]

It turns out that the human brain is deeply social. Humans aren't born loners who reluctantly learn to interact with others. Anthropology, primatology, and evolutionary studies tell us that humans are essentially group-dwelling, social beings. We are born ready to interact with and tune in to the people around us. Neural maps are involved in various aspects of tuning in to others, including imitation, understanding another's feelings/intentions, and empathy.[19]

Bodily awareness, and in particular heart and gut responses (known as interoception), may well be important in both self-compassion and empathy. In empathy, you compare what's going on in your body with what you guess is going on for others. You can't do this if you're not actually aware of your heart or gut reaction. The surprising implication is that low bodily awareness is linked to low empathy.

Empathy is an imagined process. It asks, 'Are you feeling excited? I'm feeling excited and I wonder if that's coming from my resonating with you?' Empathy involves a comparison of your intentions and feelings with those of others. The language of 'making comparison of others with oneself'[20] or 'putting oneself in another's shoes' now seems accurate to describe the process of empathy at a neurobiological level.

Like mindfulness, empathy can be cultivated. The brain is much more dynamic and malleable than was previously thought – it's still growing. By directing your attention over time, you can change the brain's structure. You aren't dependent on the quality of your childhood to have these capacities. As an adult you can use your mind to change your brain in order to benefit your whole being.

Drawing together the themes from this chapter, the message from mindfulness is that developing empathy involves both bodily awareness and broader self-awareness. These are the building blocks that enable us to sense the feelings and needs of others. The research also reminds us of the importance of practice, whether you want to develop mindfulness, empathy, or both. Directing your attention over time involves practice and repetition. The following exercise is a guided reflection that I offer in my workshops to explore and strengthen the connection between bodily awareness, self-compassion, and empathy for others. In view of the importance of practice in changing your brain, you can repeat it as many times as you want.

  ### Mindfulness, self-compassion, and empathy exercise

- Purpose of this activity: to explore experientially the connection between bodily awareness, self-compassion, and empathy for others
- Tools: somewhere to sit quietly and comfortably; a needs list, for instance the one in Appendix A; a notepad or journal and a pencil (optional)
- Time: 15 minutes

Find a place where you can sit comfortably. If you already practise a form of meditation, you could include this exercise in your regular session. If you do this practice more than once, you could consider recording the guidance, at your own pace, and playing it back as you meditate.

To help you arrive, start by bringing your attention to your body. You could start with your toes and work your way up your body to your head, and then trickle your attention down your eyes, nose, mouth, chin and throat, until you reach your chest, with your heart and lungs. Then you could follow your breathing for ten breaths.

If it helps you to become more mindfully present, you could bring your attention to what you're feeling at the moment. Start by checking in your heart, or around your heart, then lower down in your solar plexus or stomach, and higher up in your throat or even head.

When you're ready, begin by identifying the feeling that is strongest at the moment. See if you can notice where this feeling is in your body, and what it feels like (dull, dead, heavy, tight, tense, rising up, light, tingly, warm, relieving, cool, etc.).

I'll Meet You There

When you are fully in touch with the feeling, ask yourself, 'What am I longing for? What's the need underneath or behind this feeling?' Stay with this process until something shifts. The feeling may change in quality or change into another feeling. This 'shift' is a sign that you are connecting with the need, your deeper motivation. (If you get stuck, you could use a list of needs such as the one in Appendix A to identify which need is alive in you.)

When you're ready, bring to mind a close friend and recall something they said where they appeared to express a feeling, e.g. 'That's great!' or 'That was too bad!'

Try guessing what they were feeling. With 'That's great!', were they feeling pleased, relaxed, excited? With 'That was too bad!', were they feeling frustrated, annoyed, or disappointed?

When you're ready, take what they were feeling as a sign of what was important to them. What do you sense was important to them in that moment? What were they longing for? What did they need/hope for/wish for/dream of? (You could use a needs list if you get stuck.)

After 10 minutes or so, drop the exercise and sit quietly, absorbing whatever has happened. If it helps, you could make a note of the following points:

- How do you feel right now?
- What did you notice as you were doing the exercise?
- What touched you during the exercise? What did you learn from it? For instance, what was the effect of connecting with yourself before empathizing with your close friend? Did it make empathizing easier and deeper?

All living beings are terrified of punishment; all fear death. Making comparison of others with oneself, one should neither kill nor cause to kill.

– The Buddha[1]

Chapter ten

....

The ethics of empathy

Two thousand five hundred years ago, the Buddha began the process of distinguishing between human needs on the one hand and strategies on the other. Money, sex, and power are often cited as 'unhealthy' human needs. However, money wasn't a need then and isn't now. Money is a *strategy* for meeting needs – for instance, security, food, comfort, connection, and freedom. The same goes for sex. If there is a need in the area of sexual expression, it's a physical need for release. Otherwise, sex is a strategy for meeting needs, such as closeness, love, growth, belonging, play, wholeness, trust, and so on. Power is a bit more complex. Power as a need means having access to resources to meet needs. It's not a need in the sense of having 'power over' another being. When we're clear about the distinction between needs and strategies for meeting them, we can look for the needs behind any human behaviour.

Our culture, and perhaps even our religion, tells us that needs aren't spiritual, that they are selfish, egoistic, and mundane. If we want to use the language of needs, we'll have to work hard to understand the needs behind these concerns. Could it be that they arise from a doubt that the language of needs could be broad or deep enough to capture all possible meanings, especially realms of meaning and beauty where language falls short? Or perhaps from a longing to speak and act in ways that value and support the welfare of all beings? If so, it will be important to create a list of needs that includes such spiritual qualities as compassion, understanding, freedom, wholeness, and beauty.

We will also need ways to express our compassionate intention in the language of needs. In my trainings I say that it's not possible for me to meet my needs at the expense of others'.

....

Nobody's needs get met unless everybody's needs get met. I talk about honouring my own needs *and* those of the people around me. I say that my intention is compassionate connection, creating a quality of connection that will lead to everybody's needs being valued and addressed. In these ways we can keep compassion in the front and centre of our consciousness.

Compassion is by definition for everyone, including yourself. Why would you only show compassion towards others? Are you worried that you'll become selfish if you show compassion towards your own needs? There is evidence against this. Modern psychological studies suggest that people who are self-compassionate also take responsibility for their actions that cause harm.[2]

Some Buddhists tell me that the language of needs contradicts the Buddha's teachings. They argue that an Enlightened person is beyond craving, so doesn't have any needs. However, in Chapter 2 we saw that the Buddha had various needs, including peace and ease, and a longing to contribute to growth and learning, or compassion. Craving turns out to be a more complex matter. According to the Buddha, we resist our experience, trying to make pleasant experiences last and unpleasant ones go away. This craving creates most of our suffering and stress. When he became Enlightened, he noticed that, when craving stops, suffering also stops.[3]

But craving arises from ignorance. Ultimately it is ignorance, or unawareness, that keeps the wheel of samsara (un-Enlightenment) turning. Needs, by contrast, represent physical, psychological, and spiritually life-enriching resources. In this light, craving could be seen as a fixation on one particular strategy when it comes to meeting needs. More broadly, it could be seen as a lack of awareness or creativity about strategies in general, for instance how needs can be met *internally*, through inner resources, as well as *externally*, through things and people. The Buddha took meeting needs internally to new heights. He once said that he could sit quietly in meditation, finding peace and at ease, for a whole week at a time!

Does this mean that all needs are good? Understanding the needs that a person is trying to meet doesn't mean agreeing with the way they are going about meeting them. For instance, I can understand the needs that lead to states having armies – peace, security, and dignity. That doesn't mean that I accept or agree with the strategy of an army. Armies and the arms industries that supply them tend to look for work, creating suffering at home and abroad. I'm still looking for non-violent ways to bring about peace, security, and dignity.

The ethics of empathy

Remember Rumi's field, out beyond wrongdoing and rightdoing? The Buddhist tradition supports us to live in this field. The Buddha categorized actions as wholesome or unwholesome rather than good or bad. Wholesome suggests morally healthy or skilful, unwholesome its opposite. An action is wholesome or unwholesome depending on the intention or motivation from which it comes. The Buddha regarded actions based on greed, hatred, and ignorance as unwholesome and predicted that they would lead to suffering for oneself and others. By contrast, he regarded actions based on generosity, love, and awareness as wholesome, and predicted that they would lead to happiness for oneself and others. This is the ethics of intention.

Usually the ethics of intention and the ethics of empathy are regarded as two separate ways of measuring ethics. However, they are related. Skilful awareness is an aspect of a wholesome intention. You need to be aware of your motivations and the likely consequences of actions, in particular their impact on others' well-being. In order to predict the likely effects of your actions on other people, you need a sense of connection and imagination. As the fourteenth Dalai Lama points out in a book on ethics, this is where empathy comes in. Connection enables you to see the life in other beings. Imagination enables you to think and experience what it's like to be the other person: to put yourself in their shoes, to see with their eyes. If you cannot imagine the potential impact of your actions on others, then you have no means to discriminate between what is wholesome and what is unwholesome, between what is harmful and what is not.[4]

So ethics is not simply a matter of wholesome or unwholesome, black or white. The more of this kind of imagination you have, the more you are able to act in a morally healthy way. As with any skill, it comes with practice and experience. In the language of needs, wholesomeness is when you learn how to meet your own needs in ways that embody a compassionate awareness of the needs of those around you.

Stories illustrating this aspect of ethics are more often associated with the Mahayana schools of Buddhism, which emphasize compassion. However, there are a number of passages in the earlier Pali scriptures that provide a concrete and specific sense of empathy. First among these is the touching story of the conversation between King Pasenadi of Kosala and Queen Mallikā. The two of them were sitting on the upper terrace of their palace. This was at a time when brick-built buildings were rare and multi-storeyed buildings even rarer.

The king turned to his queen and asked, 'Mallikā, is there anyone dearer to you than yourself?' The word used here for 'self' is *attan*. It was used in everyday speech and most often simply meant 'myself, yourself', with no implications of a metaphysical 'Self'.

Queen Mallikā replies, 'Your Majesty, there is no one dearer to me than myself. And you, sire, is anyone dearer to you than yourself?'

Pasenadi replies, 'It's the same for me. There is no one dearer to me, Mallikā, than myself.'

When this conversation had sunk in, Pasenadi went down from the palace to where the Buddha was staying in Sāvatthī, and reported the conversation. The Buddha appreciated King Pasenadi and Queen Mallikā's insight, and spoke this verse:

> Though in thought we range throughout the world,
> We'll nowhere find a thing more dear than self.
> So, since others hold the self so dear,
> He who loves himself should injure none.[5]

The king and queen see through the illusion of their royal status and have an empathic insight. They realize that, for each of them, the dearest person in the universe is ... themselves. By the same token they recognize that other people are dearest to themselves. The Buddha confirms this with a verse: nothing is dearer in the universe than oneself. This applies to everyone. Recognizing this, if you love yourself, you will also love others and avoid harming them.

This story makes it clear that the basis for acting ethically is our capacity to (i) connect with the beings around us, and (ii) imagine the potential impact of our actions. This is the ethics of empathy.

Generalizing from this, the Buddha said:

> All (living beings) are terrified of punishment; all fear death. Making comparison (of others) with oneself, one should neither kill nor cause to kill.

> All (living beings) are terrified of punishment; to all, life is dear. Making comparison (of others) with oneself, one should neither kill nor cause to kill.[6]

The ethics of empathy is a process of reflectively comparing our experience to that of others. We're terrified of punishment and fear death. Looking around, we notice that other sentient beings seem to be alive and conscious in the same way as us. We also notice how much effort goes into avoiding punishment and death. From this we conclude that all sentient beings share our fears. When we make this comparison, killing another being becomes unthinkable.

There seem to be two types of comparison: *invidious* and *empathic*. Invidious means creating resentment or envy. We compare ourselves with another person, focusing on the differences between us, and find that one of us is superior. In this regard I remember a story that Urgyen Sangharakshita told of his time as a young sadhu wandering around India in the early 1950s. One of his encounters was with a fearsome but deeply compassionate one-eyed guru:

> Since there were two different forms of egotism, pride and humility, he had two different methods of dealing with people. With those who were proud he behaved more proudly still; with those who were humble, with even greater humility. Thus both were made to realize

how egotistic they actually were. 'However high you go,' he concluded, addressing me directly, 'I shall always be above you. However low you go, I shall always be below you.' The idea that humility was just as much a form of egotism as pride represented an important new insight for me, and I never forgot the swami's words.[7]

Invidious comparison involves seeing yourself as better than or above others, or worse than and below others. We can add a third type: regarding yourself as equal to others. In the *Sutta Nipāta*, one of the oldest records of the Buddha's teaching, there is a description of the ideal monk: 'He has to avoid thinking of himself as better, or worse than, or equal to anyone.'[8] The Buddhist scriptures are nothing if not thorough! By contrast, empathic comparison is when you compare yourself to others with the focus on shared experiences, hopes, dreams, values, needs, and deeper motivations.

This empathic reflection became the first precept or ethical training principle of Buddhism. It is the cornerstone of non-violence. Usually it is phrased in terms of what *not* to do: 'I undertake the training principle to abstain from taking life.' However, it can also be formulated in terms or what you *will* do: 'With deeds of loving-kindness, I purify my body.'

We can even extend our imaginative empathy to the natural world. Sangharakshita encourages his students not to limit their empathic imagination to living organisms. You can extend it even to inorganic matter or natural events. He argues that it's important for us to rediscover this capacity for empathy with the life around us, because this is the true basis of ethics.[9]

Living in cities and surrounded by technology, it is difficult to maintain a sense of solidarity with life. We are much more likely to experience it in a forest or other natural place. But, whether we live in a city or a forest, we need to remember that 'The natural world is alive, full of life that resonates with our own lives and is valuable as life.'[10] For some people, involvement in environmental action is motivated by this ethics of empathy. For others, involvement in science is a way of manifesting it. The Native American Iroquois have a saying:

I'll Meet You There

In every deliberation, we must consider the impact on the seventh generation ... even if it requires having skin as thick as the bark of a pine... What about the seventh generation? Where are you taking them? What will they have?[11]

In the same way that empathy is the basis for acting ethically, it is also the basis for the emotional attitude of compassion. The Buddha taught that compassion is one of four brahma vihāras or 'divine abidings'. These are universal loving-kindness, compassion, empathic joy, and equanimity. Loving-kindness is fundamental, and transforms into compassion when it comes into contact with suffering, empathic joy when it encounters joy, and equanimity when it faces both suffering and joy together. Empathy runs through all of them. Inasmuch as loving-kindness and compassion entail acting, they could be described as the active dimension of empathy.

Empathy is the basis of compassion. In 2016 I co-led a post-earthquake trauma-healing event in Nepal. In the following exercise, try to sense the feelings and needs behind Savithri's words.

 Empathy exercise

- Purpose of this activity: to identify the feelings and needs behind the words of the speaker
- Tools: a notepad or journal and a pencil
- Time: 5–10 minutes

For each of the sentences in italics, try to identify the speaker's feelings and needs. If you want, you can compare your guesses with mine at the end. As before, bear in mind that there are no right answers.

Savithri is a thirty-year-old woman from the Nuwakot region of Nepal. She wears a dark red woollen jumper and skirt, the traditional dress for married women. She wants to talk about what happened in the recent earthquake.

(*In a quiet, monotonous voice*) It was a Saturday, *so my husband and I were lucky we were outside*, working in our field. We felt the tremors, but we often

---

get them, *so we thought that they would just go away*. They just got stronger and stronger, *until the earth was shaking and throwing us down*. I tried to run back into the house to check if there was anyone inside, but I kept on falling down. The roof of the house collapsed. We lost our goats, just swallowed up into the earth. *That was a bad thing for us*. When the tremors subsided I went back inside to tidy things up, but everything was thrown all over the place, here and there. *I felt despair*. But *I was mainly worried about my daughter*, who lives in another village. I tried calling her, but the phones didn't work. I went with my husband on his motorbike to her village. *The roads were very bad*. We got there, and found the house where my daughter was staying. The roof had collapsed. *The neighbours told us that she had been taken to hospital*. We drove to the hospital and found her. She was lying in bed. (pause) *She had been injured*. (pause) *I was so worried for her*. While we were there, my husband got a call to say that our aunt and uncle had been killed. (*Savithri goes silent*.)

I suggest you cover up my guesses below and make a note of your own guesses about Savithri's feelings and needs. Then, if you like, compare them to my guesses.

My guesses

In a quiet, monotonous voice. As soon as I heard Savithri's tone of voice I could guess that she was feeling numb, possibly still in shock.

So my husband and I were lucky we were outside. I guessed that Savithri felt relieved because she needed safety for herself and those she loved.

So we thought that they would just go away. Savithri and her husband felt relaxed initially, needing ease.

Until the earth was shaking and throwing us down. Savithri starts to feel fear, then panic, and she needs safety for those she loves and her belongings.

That was a bad thing for us. Savithri is reconnecting with a sense of loss and sadness. She needs safety and protection.

I felt despair. Now Savithri is telling us directly how she felt.

I was mainly worried about my daughter. Again she is feeling panicky because she wants safety and protection for those she loves.

The roads were very bad. Savithri is feeling frustrated, longing for ease. She's also feeling scared, needing safety.

I'll Meet You There

The neighbours told us that she had been taken to hospital. Savithri's feeling increases to full-blown panic. She needs clarity about the severity of the situation, and safety.

She had been injured. Savithri is feeling shocked, needing awareness that this could happen. Also dread, because she wants those she loves to be safe.

Savithri goes silent. She's feeling overwhelmed, and needs space to mourn. She needs space to honour and dignify the lives of those she has lost.

I remain silent, sitting next to her. After 10 minutes, she looks up at me. In a firmer voice she thanks me for giving her space to be heard. It's 'what she's always wanted'.

Monks, there is one person who was born and comes into the world for the welfare and happiness of the people, out of compassion (*anukampā*) for the world, for the benefit, welfare, and happiness of gods and human beings. Who is that person? The [Buddha], the Worthy One, the fully and completely Enlightened one.

– The Buddha[1]

Chapter eleven

···

The empathic Buddha

At first glance, there doesn't seem to be a specific term for empathy in the Buddhist texts. However, the above traditional description of the Buddha comes close. *Anukampā* has a surprising meaning. The word is usually translated as 'compassion', however its etymology is as an action noun with the root *kamp*, which means 'tremble' and the prefix *anu*, which means 'following'. So it means 'trembling with' even 'resonating with'. The passage suggests that the Buddha trembles with or resonates with the world, for the benefit, welfare, and happiness of gods and human beings. The Buddha senses the experience of all beings. He feels it in his body. He's not separate. So *anukampā* is used as a word to describe the heart/mind of an Enlightened being, and it comes closest to what is meant by empathy at the level of Enlightenment.

Empathy is also represented symbolically in the story of the Buddha's vision of beings as lotuses from Chapter 2. As a result of his Enlightenment, Gautama developed the *buddhacakkhu* or 'Buddha eye', a kind of non-physical, spiritual vision. With this mystical eye he looked out over humanity and saw lotus flowers at different stages of development. He recognized everyone's spiritual potential, and it was on this account that he decided to teach the Dharma. And, as we discovered in Chapter 9, the Buddha saw empathy as an integral part of mindfulness – a mindful awareness of others and our communication with them.

The three Anuruddhas

The Buddha encouraged his disciples to live together in empathic community. One of the most delightful examples of this kind of communal harmony comes in the story of the three

Anuruddhas.[2] One evening after meditating, the Buddha goes to visit three of his disciples: Anuruddha, Nandiya, and Kimbila. They are living in retreat in the Gosinga park. The park keeper sees the Buddha and tells him not to enter and disturb the three monks. This unexpected detail implies something interesting: to the park keeper, the Buddha was indistinguishable from other monks wearing faded yellow robes. Fortunately, Anuruddha sees the Buddha talking to the park keeper and recognizes his teacher, 'the Blessed One'. He calls his two companions, and the three of them welcome the Buddha. They bow down respectfully, sit down, and wait for him to speak.

The Buddha is concerned about their physical well-being. Are they are in good health, are they comfortable, are they getting enough alms food from the village to live on? The answer is yes.

Then the Buddha checks how they are getting on together, as a community. Are they living in harmony? Do they appreciate each other? Are they free from disputes? Are they blending together like milk and water, looking at each other with kindness in their eyes? Again, the answer is yes.

The Buddha wants to know how they do it. Anuruddha tells him that they practise on the level of intention. They remind themselves of the benefits of living together with other spiritual practitioners. They act with loving-kindness in body, speech, and mind towards each other. They do this both in public and in private. They value each other deeply and are willing to contribute to the collective welfare. Anuruddha concludes by saying, 'We are different in body, venerable sir, but one in mind.'[3] Nandiya and Kimbila confirm this.

Once the Buddha has assured himself about their physical comfort and communal harmony, he asks them about their spiritual practice. Are they getting on with their spiritual practice, mindfully, ardently, and resolutely? Yes, Anuruddha replies. But how do they do this?

Surprisingly, Anuruddha responds by giving some of the practical details of their life. The community is woven together by empathy and mindfulness. Every morning they go for their alms round in the village. Whoever gets back first puts out the seats, the water for drinking and washing, and the refuse bucket. Whoever gets back last eats any leftovers. If he doesn't want the leftovers, he throws them somewhere where there is no vegetation or drops them into water where there is no life. This detail suggests the early Buddhists' deep mindfulness of their environment. To complete the cycle, the last person puts away the water, the seats, and the refuse bucket, and sweeps the dining room. At any time, if someone notices that the water for washing, for drinking, or for the toilets is low, he takes care of it. If something is too heavy for him, he signals with his hand to one of the others to help him. Every five days they sit through the night discussing the Buddha's teaching. That's how they do it.

The Buddha is pleased to hear this. He goes on to ask them about their meditation practice. Have they experienced the *jhāna*s (Sanskrit *dhyāna*s)? These are deep and subtle meditational states. Anuruddha says yes, they have. In fact they have experienced all eight *jhāna*s, and even attained a state of purity, freedom, and wisdom. The Buddha confirms that they have reached the highest state of consciousness.

Now this has been established, the Buddha gets up and leaves. The three companions accompany him a little way then head back to their huts. Once in the hut, Nandiya and Kimbila ask Anuruddha if they have ever told him about their attainments. He says no, they haven't. But by reaching out to their minds with his mind, he knows their state of consciousness. 'We are different in body, venerable sir, but one in mind.'

The Anuruddhas represent the ideal spiritual community. They appreciate each other and are free from disputes. They blend together like milk and water, looking at each other with kindness in their eyes. When asked about their practice, they give a detailed picture of how they live together, including their ecological awareness. The Buddha demonstrates his deep care for his disciples, first in visiting them and second through his questions about their physical and spiritual welfare.

The Buddha wants to know what is important to them and how. The three cultivate gratitude towards each other, and all are willing to contribute to the collective welfare by taking the other person's perspective. And Anuruddha, at least, seems to have a spiritual empathy for his companions' state of consciousness. All these details suggest empathic community – living in harmony with each other and the environment.

The monk with dysentery

But what happens when this kind of empathy for one another gets lost? At another time, the Buddha was on a tour of his monks' lodgings with his attendant Ānanda. The Buddha looked into one of the rooms and saw a monk lying on the floor. He was fouled in his own urine and excrement. The Buddha approached him and asked what was wrong. The monk replied that he had dysentery (a kind of gastroenteritis). The Buddha asked, did he have an attendant to look after him? No, he said. The Buddha was puzzled, 'Then why aren't your fellow monks looking after you?'

'They don't look after me, Lord, because I don't do anything for them.'

The Buddha was rather taken aback to hear this. But, instead of going first to talk to the other monks, he turned to Ānanda and said, 'Ānanda, go and fetch some water. We will wash this monk.'

The Buddha sprinkled water on the monk and Ānanda washed it off. When this was done, the Buddha took him by the head, and Ānanda by the feet, and they lifted him back onto his bed.

Later the Buddha called all the monks together. First he checked things out, asking if they were aware that there was a sick monk living in their midst, with dysentery and without an attendant. They replied that they were aware of this. So the Buddha asked, 'Then why don't you monks look after him?'

They replied, 'We don't look after him, Lord, because he doesn't do anything for us.'

The Buddha was again taken aback, and said, 'Monks, now that you have left home and become my followers, you have no mother or father to look after you. If you don't look after one another, who will look after you? Whoever wishes to look after me should look after the sick.'[4]

Perhaps it's not surprising that Jesus said something similar in St Matthew's Gospel:

> For I was hungry, and you gave me something to eat. I was thirsty, and you gave me something to drink. I was a stranger, and you welcomed me. I was naked, and you clothed me. I was sick, and you took care of me. I was in prison, and you visited me. ... Truly I tell you, in that you did it for one of the least important of these my brothers, you did it for me.[5]

The Buddha reminds the monks that it is an offence against the *Vinaya*, or monastic code, not to look after someone who is sick. He finishes by talking about the attributes and pitfalls of being a sick person and a caregiver. In this way the Buddha undertakes and spells out the responsibilities of empathic community in times of sickness.

Conflict is inevitable, violence isn't

Conflict arises through differences of temperament, culture, and belief, and in relation to resources. I would say that it's inevitable. Violence is a common way of dealing with conflict. However, it's not inevitable in the same way as conflict is. When I'm preparing to mediate between Israelis and Palestinians, or Sinhalese and Tamils in Sri Lanka, I remind myself that conflict is inevitable, violence isn't. This reminds me that I'm not trying to do away with conflict. And it helps me to focus on what I *can* do: repair connections and find non-violent ways to respond to conflict.

Things were no different in the Buddha's lifetime. There were numerous wars between the local republics and kingdoms. Five years after his Enlightenment, the Buddha visited his home town, Kapilavastu, in the foothills of the Himalayas. A dispute had arisen between the Śākyans from Kapilavastu and their Koliyan neighbours.[6] As it happens, the Buddha was related to the Koliyans as well, through his mother, so both sides were his relatives.

The Śākyans and Koliyans had collaborated in building a dam on the river Rohini, which ran between their tribal territories. But this year the sun was hot and the crops were already beginning to droop. It looked like there wouldn't be enough water in the dam to irrigate the fields on both sides. The slave-labourers on both sides got together to discuss the situation. The Koliyan labourers said, 'There isn't enough water to irrigate both sides. Our crops will ripen with a single watering so let us have the water.'

The Śākyan labourers replied, 'It's beneath our dignity to come begging to you when your storehouses are full and ours are empty. Our crops will also ripen with a single watering, so let us have the water.' Neither side was prepared to give in. Tempers flared until one labourer got up and hit a labourer from the other side. The labourer returned the punch and there was a fight.

During the fight the Koliyans started badmouthing the Śākyan royal family, accusing them of co-habiting with their own sisters, like dogs and jackals. The Śākyan labourers replied by calling the Koliyans lepers and accusing them of living in the hollows of trees like animals.

Both groups of labourers went and reported the fight to the ministers in charge of farming, and the ministers reported it to the royal families. When the royals heard the insults that had been flung, they armed themselves for battle. Riding forth from their palaces in their chariots, the Śākyans cried, 'We will show you the strength and power of those who have co-habited with their sisters.' And the Koliyans cried, 'We will show you the strength and power of those who live in trees.'

So one fine morning the Buddha turned up just as the tribes were squaring up. He quickly realized that if he didn't intervene they would kill each other. So he went and sat down mindfully between the two battle lines. When the kings and princes saw the Buddha they threw down their spears, bows, and swords, and respectfully bowed towards him. The Buddha asked the royals on both sides, 'What is this dispute about, great kings?' They couldn't tell him. So he asked the commanders-in-chief of the armies, but they couldn't tell him either. Eventually the Buddha asked the slave-labourers, and they told him, 'The dispute is over water, your holiness.'

Once he'd established this, the Buddha went back to the kings and asked, 'How much is water worth, great kings?'

'Very little, your holiness.'

'And how much are warrior-princes worth, great kings?'

'Warrior-princes are invaluable, your holiness.'

'It seems out of proportion that you're willing to destroy invaluable warrior-princes for a little water.'

The kings and their princes went silent. The Buddha talked to them about the benefits of transforming hatred and greed, and after a while the two sides turned their chariots round and went back to their palaces.

The build-up to this fifth-century BCE conflict could be the model for countless wars and international incidents. The initial trigger is a difficulty over shared resources, in this case water. This was at a time when the world population was a tiny fraction of what it is today, the climate in India was more benign, and natural resources were abundant. Today the world's population is thousands of times larger, the climate is warming up, and natural resources such as virgin forest and crude oil are dwindling. How many times have you heard of wars being fought over rich colonies or, more recently, oil supplies? It seems likely that, as the population increases and natural resources dwindle, these kinds of conflicts can only increase.

The conflict over irrigation raises issues of dignity for both the Śākyan and the Koliyan slave-labourers. Neither side is willing to go begging for food later in the season. Neither side gets heard for its desire for dignity and self-determination. This leads to irritation. There is a flashpoint when one person throws a punch. Perhaps he's settling an old grudge. Once these two people are fighting, others join in. During the fight, existing 'enemy images' surface again. These enemy images deny the humanity of the other tribe, comparing them to animals. What are modern comparisons? 'Imperialist', 'terrorist', 'racist', 'murderer', 'suicide bomber', and of course the labels of 'Jewish', 'Muslim', 'Christian', 'American', 'Western', and so on, which have become enemy images in themselves.

When these enemy images come to the attention of the warrior-princes, their immediate response is to arm themselves and prepare for battle. It's possible to guess that beneath their pride is a wish to protect the reputation of their tribe. And underneath this, perhaps a desperate longing for dignity and self-respect. But again, they don't know how to resolve conflict without recourse to violence.

When the Buddha sits between the battle lines, the first thing he does is try to understand the trigger for the conflict. Ironically, no one knows what it is. Only the slave-labourers who were initially involved can tell him it's about water. Then the Buddha asks the kings what is deeply important to them – the lives of warrior-princes or water?

It's a searching, empathic question that leads both sides to consider what is most valuable to them. They realize that their deepest need is to protect their lives. They see that their present course of action is very likely to be harmful. And they start looking for another course of action that is less harmful.

This happens time and again in mediations between two people or groups. When the two sides are fully heard, the conflict that appeared to be between them just melts away. Each party recognizes a deeper truth about themselves. In the case of the Śākyans and Koliyans, they realize the importance of protecting their lives. In the light of this, external conflict no longer seems relevant.

The Buddha might have asked the two sides if it was a matter of dignity to them, and they would probably have said yes. However, he chose to connect with their deepest need first and the result was that they fell silent and went home. Conflict is inevitable, violence isn't. Try to sense the feelings and needs behind the words of these two people in conflict.

Empathy exercise

- Purpose of this activity: to identify the feelings and needs behind the words of each speaker, without getting caught up in their thoughts
- Tools: a notepad or journal and a pencil
- Time: 5–10 minutes

For each of the sentences in italics, try to sense what is important to the speaker. If you want, you can compare your guesses with mine at the end.

Jack and Diane are a couple who have come for mediation and counselling. One of their flare-up points is when Jack is driving and doesn't know the route. Notice whose side you take – men and women tend to adopt different approaches.

Jack: Don't start on that topic!

Diane: I'll start if I'm minded to. *You can't stop me.*

Jack: *You know where this is heading.*

Diane: That's the point. You don't know where we're heading, and *you don't care.* You would just keep driving until we crashed into the sea.

Jack: *I can't believe this.*

Diane: *You'd have thought that having a map on your phone would make you more likely to use it.*

Jack: *What are road signs for? Besides, the screen is too small.*

Diane: Well do it the old-fashioned way and look at a map.

Jack: We're retired. We can drive around a little until we find it. *Besides, we might see something different.*

Diana: *I've had it with you. You're not human.*

Make a note of your own guesses about what is important to each speaker. Then, if you like, compare them to my guesses below.

My guesses

You can't stop me. Diane is feeling frustrated because she wants freedom, and to be heard fully.

You know where this is heading. Jack is afraid of losing what connection and closeness they have.

You don't care. Diane is feeling hurt because she wants to matter, she wants her feelings to be taken into account.

I can't believe this. Jack is getting scared and maybe angry now. He wants to protect himself and the partnership.

You'd have thought that having a map on your phone would make you more likely to use it. Diane is feeling irritated because she'd like understanding for her fear and discomfort when Jack doesn't know the route.

What are road signs for? Besides, the screen is too small. Jack is feeling frustrated and wants slack to find his own way.

Besides, we might see something different. Jack actually enjoys not knowing where he is going; it gives him a sense of adventure and freshness.

I've had it with you. You're not human. Diane is feeling very angry and wants understanding. She is also feeling deeply hurt and needs to protect herself.

How did you get on? This is a realistic mediation situation. Could you stay in the car with them and take both sides? Or did you end up thinking that one side was rather foolish? If a judgement came like this, I suggest that you make a note of it and do some self-empathy on it. What are you feeling when this judgement enters your mind? And what are the needs behind this feeling? This kind of self-empathy will give you the resilience to mediate in similar situations in the future.

As long as space abides and as long as the world abides, so long may I abide, destroying the sufferings of the world.

– Śāntideva[1]

Chapter twelve

....

The moon at the window

In the seventh and eighth century CE, an Indian Buddhist monk called Śāntideva wrote *The Bodhicaryāvatāra* or *Guide to the Buddhist Path to Awakening*. The poem explores the intense aspiration to act altruistically. At the heart of the poem is the figure of the bodhisattva, one who has generated the *bodhicitta* or Awakening Mind. The *bodhicitta* is the intention to work for the benefit of all beings right up to Buddhahood. The fourteenth Dalai Lama has frequently cited the above verse of the *Bodhicaryāvatāra* as his greatest aspiration. He is also quoted as saying:

> If I have any understanding of compassion and the
> practice of the bodhisattva path, it is entirely on the basis
> of this text that I possess it.[2]

In chapter 8 of the *Bodhicaryāvatāra*, Śāntideva examines the principle of putting oneself in the place of another. Here again the ethics of empathy are at work. He also describes two meditation practices for bringing this principle alive. These are 'equalizing self and others' and 'exchanging self and others'. While we're exploring these practices, it's worth remembering that they were regarded as advanced insight practices, handed down in private from teacher to disciple!

The preliminary to each of them is to become absorbed in meditation and develop a calm mind. Once this is established, Śāntideva instructs us to meditate intently on the equality of oneself and others as follows, by saying to ourselves, 'All equally experience suffering and happiness. I should look after them as I do myself.'[3]

Śāntideva's argument is that a body is divided into different limbs, but you protect it as a single entity. Similarly, though the world is divided into different beings, you need to protect it as a single entity. Another person's suffering and stress is hard for *them* to bear because they love themselves. As you love yourself, and recognizing other people as 'selves', why don't you also find other people's suffering and stress intolerable?

He invites us to continue:

> I should dispel the suffering of others because it is suffering like my own suffering. I should help others too because of their nature as beings, which is like my own being.[4]

And later he invites us to consider that:

> Without exception, no sufferings belong to anyone. They must be warded off simply because they are suffering. Why is any limitation put on this?[5]

So the practice of equalizing self and others invites you to value yourself and others equally. This means to care equally for both – to alleviate the suffering and stress of others as you do your own. It is a practice that will support you in developing compassion. In terms of human needs, it could be put like this: needs are just needs – it doesn't matter whose they are. They are all important, and we want to find ways to meet them.

The second practice of exchanging self and other is described as the supreme mystery.[6] Could you imagine exchanging your happiness for the suffering and stress of other beings? It's not for the faint-hearted! I suggest that you only consider doing this if you have already developed a strong sense of self-confidence and loving-kindness (or *mettā*). In the first stage of the practice, Śāntideva suggests that you imagine yourself in the shoes of someone else. Choose a person who thinks they are *inferior* to you in some way – someone who is envious of you. You can even imagine what they might be thinking about you... You are honoured and praised. People give you gifts while the inferior person doesn't receive gifts and is criticized. You seem to be famous and well respected while they do menial work, and seem to be inferior.

In the second stage of the practice, imagine exchanging places with someone who is a *competitive rival*. You can imagine their thoughts... You promote yourself at the cost of conflict... If their own virtues were better known, there would be no praise for you... In the end you will become the object of everyone's ridicule.

In the third stage, you can imagine exchanging places with someone who regards themselves as *superior* to you. Listen to their thoughts... They have far more learning, wisdom, beauty, good breeding, and wealth than you... You don't deserve anything except just enough food to live on... You must be punished.

In the fourth and final stage, you imagine exchanging places with other kinds of people. Like them, you can turn against yourself. Every unkind act you've done to others, now you can do to yourself. You can even get jealous of yourself or point out your faults. Whatever you did maliciously to others to benefit yourself, you put yourself in the same predicament for the benefit of all beings.[7]

Shantideva offers us strong medicine to help us enlarge our capacity to empathize with those around us and develop the 'ethics of empathy'.

Compassion requires empathic understanding

Compassionate activity is underpinned by an empathic understanding of what beings really need. Do you remember, in Chapter 1, the monkeys who didn't know how to help younger monkeys cross the stream? We need to be able to see things from another person's side in order to help them. In Buddhism this insight is depicted through the Bhavacakra or Wheel of Life, a cosmic diagram especially popular in Tibet (see Figure 4).

The Buddha grew up with the idea that the universe consisted of a number of realms. On the eve of his Enlightenment, the Buddha-to-be reflected on how beings were reborn. Depending on their actions (*kamma*, Sanskrit *karma*), they were reborn in different realms.[8] In the Bhavacakra or Wheel of Life, there are six realms: the gods, the titans (angry gods), hungry ghosts, hell beings, animals, and humans.

If you look closely, you'll notice that a Buddha figure appears in each realm.[9] The Buddha is offering something specific

Fig. 4 The Wheel of Life.

that will benefit the beings in that realm. He brings together a generous impulse with an empathic understanding of what would really benefit those beings. So what does the Buddha give in each realm?

In the god realm, the beings can see heaven opening before their eyes! It is a world of pleasures and delights, beautiful gardens and palaces, trees and fountains. Here a pure-white Buddha holds a *vina* – a musical instrument like a lute. On this instrument he plays a sweet and penetrating melody, the melody of impermanence. The message of the lute is that nothing lasts – everything is like the previous moment of a ball of foam. Of course, the gods don't know that this is the teaching they need. They believe that their state is eternal, and it certainly seems like that. They are lost in the unmindfulness of bliss. But one day things will start to change, and the melody of impermanence gives them some forewarning of this. The Buddha can sense that they are only open to something of great beauty, with a subtle message.

In the world of the titans (angry gods), the males are fierce, war-like beings, heavily armed and engaged in perpetual battle. The females are depicted as thin and beautiful, like supermodels! The Buddha in this realm is a beautiful emerald green. He holds aloft a flaming sword. This is the sword of transcendental wisdom, which he brandishes at the titans as they fight. They can recognize him because, like them, he is wielding a sword. However, his sword has a different meaning. It cuts through the unmindfulness that leads the titans to believe that everybody is out to get them, and that the only way to survive is to strike first. The Buddha has empathic insight into their state of mind, and how to meet and transform it.

In the third realm are the hungry ghosts or *preta*s. These are naked and horribly deformed. They've got swollen bellies, thin necks, and tiny mouths. They suffer from ravenous hunger as they desperately try to cram food into their tiny mouths. What food they manage to get in turns into excrement and liquid fire. From a psychological perspective, the beings are unaware of their addictions and what would really nourish them. A beautiful ruby-red Buddha showers the *preta*s with food and drink that they can actually consume. Eating this food, the hungry ghosts can nourish themselves without harm. The Buddha's empathic insight comes in knowing that they need nourishment, and what kinds of food and drink can sustain them.

In the fourth realm, at the bottom of the circle, you can see the hell realm. This is the world of tormented beings. Some of them are suffering torments so terrible that you can hardly bear to think about them, much less describe them. The realm is filled with the stench of burning human flesh and the screams of tortured souls. The inhabitants are simply unmindful, being tormented and distracted by their suffering. However, the bluish-grey Buddha doesn't just offer meditation to them. With an arm on fire, it's going to be difficult for them to sit still long enough to develop mindfulness! With an empathic understanding of the intensity of their suffering, the Buddha offers them nectar, the food of the gods, which provides some respite from the pain. Perhaps the respite is long enough for them to reflect on how they got there and what they might do differently in future.

Continuing round the Bhavacakra, you see the world of animals, both domesticated and wild. They are usually shown in mating pairs, grazing, and living a very peaceful, idyllic existence. Perhaps this is how it appears from the animals' point of view. Animals don't know what's going to happen tomorrow, and don't think about it. They just live for today, happily and peacefully. In the world of the animals, the beings are unaware of the possibility of choosing a different kind of life. A deep-blue Buddha is showing a book to them. He empathically understands that basically they are content, and that they might get interested in learning and culture, which would allow them to develop greater self-awareness.

Finally, in the sixth segment you can see the human realm. Here human beings are going about their daily business. You see them buying, selling, reading, talking, having children, and finally being taken as corpses to the cremation ground. They are unaware of the possibility of Enlightenment. In this realm there is a yellow Buddha in saffron robes carrying a begging bowl and a staff. He symbolizes the possibility of a spiritual life. He understands that humans are on the whole occupied with their everyday tasks, and that they might be open to searching for a truth that gives them a deeper meaning.

The Buddhas in the six realms represent the emergence of great compassion in the Wheel of Life. With an empathic awareness of the states of mind of the inhabitants, they are able to give something that will really alleviate suffering and stress, and support spiritual development.

A genius for connection

There is a story from Japan about the poet Ryōkan, one of the most beloved of the Japanese Zen masters. Ryōkan wrote poems celebrating mindfulness and the simple life of a hermit. He also had a genius for connection with people of all ages and occupations.

Ryōkan lived in a little hut at the foot of a mountain. One evening while he was out, a thief came to his hut. Because Ryōkan led a very simple life, the thief found nothing to steal. Ryōkan returned and surprised the thief, but the thief needn't have worried. Instead of scolding him, Ryōkan said, 'You have come a long way and I wouldn't like you to return empty-handed. Please take my clothes with you as a gift.' The thief was confused. Nevertheless, he took the clothes and went away.

Ryōkan sat naked in his hut watching the moon. He reflected, 'I would have liked to have helped him more. If only I could have given him this beautiful moon.'[10]

We could leave the story there, in its beauty and simplicity. However, there may be value in exploring it. Ryōkan lived a very simple life. He owned very little, and begged for his food in the local village. He seems to have been happy like this. Instead of giving him a sense of poverty, his simple circumstances seem to have helped him develop generosity. When the thief comes to call, Ryōkan treats him as a visitor, and can only think of the long trip he must have made. It would be a waste of a trip for him to leave empty-handed. Perhaps the man has children to feed. Ryōkan wants to support him. If he has come a long way and is prepared to risk harm and even injury in robbing other people's houses, he must really need help. Ryōkan has nothing that the man can carry so he offers his clothes. He gives him what he has.

Zen masters are known for their completely unexpected responses, and Ryōkan is no exception. It's a potentially difficult and dangerous situation, with nothing to steal and a cornered thief. Ryōkan disarms the thief by enquiring after his welfare and offering his own clothes. Later he wishes he could have helped more, by giving him an experience of peace and beauty. The moon symbolizes Ryōkan's deep meditative experience. It belongs to no one and no one can give or steal it.

Ryōkan is implicitly connected with the people around him. He feels this connection even with a man whose intention is to rob him. Ryōkan cuts through such thoughts as 'This man is a thief... Thieves are bad... They should be punished', to the needs of the situation. If the man has come a long way, risking harm and injury, he clearly needs all the support he can get. It is Ryōkan's generosity, coupled with his extraordinary ability to connect with people and see things from their perspective, that leads him to act in the way he does.

  Empathy exercise

- Purpose of this activity: to explore your connection with all beings through shared responses to happiness and suffering or stress
- Tools: somewhere to sit quietly and comfortably, a notepad or journal and a pencil (optional)
- Time: 15 minutes

Connect with yourself (your body, feelings, and thoughts), and remind yourself of your compassionate intention, however you do or say that for yourself. You might look at a picture of a compassionate figure, or call that figure to mind. You could say, 'Going for connection, hanging loose to the outcome' silently to yourself.

When you are ready, reflect that all humans are interconnected. There is nothing fixed or permanent in the universe. You can never step into the same river twice, as the ancient Greek philosopher Heraclitus said. You are part of that process. All beings are part of that process. No one remains the same.

I'll Meet You There

If it supports you to connect and to contribute to life, reflect on what we have in common: all beings want to be happy and avoid suffering and stress. Call to mind a specific instance of your own stress and imagine or call to mind other people experiencing the same kind of stress. For example, if you suffer from backache, call to mind or imagine other people who suffer from backache. Do the same for a specific thing that you are happy about. Try to get a sense that these are real human beings who are experiencing stress and happiness, just as real as you.

And behind this stress and happiness, try to get a sense of what these beings are longing for. Try to sense what would benefit yourself and others. Perhaps a sense of ease or peace, or freedom, or a sense of meaning, or compassion, or understanding, or being understood?

Notice your response to doing this. Notice what you are feeling and what needs of yours are alive. If 'enemy images' of yourself or others come up, rather than pushing them away, in this exercise try to find the needs behind these judgements. For example, if you are thinking, 'I'm no good at this!', are you feeling discouraged, because you would really like to be in touch with your sense of compassion? If you are thinking, 'They don't deserve my compassion!', are you frustrated, because you really value awareness that actions have consequences? And so on.

After 10 minutes, pause and give yourself space to absorb the exercise. You might like to sit quietly with a cup of tea or make some notes in your journal. What touched you during the exercise? What did you learn?

Part 4

Drawing the threads together

And did you get what
you wanted from this life, even so?

I did.

And what did you want?

To call myself beloved, to feel myself
beloved on the earth.

– Raymond Carver[1]

Chapter thirteen

....

Empathy in children

Understanding how empathy develops in children draws together various threads of this book. It's important to realize that in most children empathy develops quite naturally around the age of two years.[2] But in some children the capacity to empathize comes later, or never fully develops. For instance, children who are diagnosed as having autistic spectrum disorder (ASD) or as being 'schizophrenic' appear to have a reduced capacity for empathy. Autism has been described as an 'empathy disorder',[3] although the reduced capacity might well arise from a deeper lack of attention to the people around. What we can say with some confidence is that people with an ASD diagnosis haven't practised paying attention to those around them as much as people without autism. Studies suggest that children with an ASD diagnosis are less sensitive to social cues, and have a reluctance to look at other people's eyes and less interest in or sensitivity to the voice of someone speaking to them.[4]

There is a mild form of autism known as Asperger's syndrome. One study brought together a group of participants diagnosed with Asperger's who scored lower than the control group on cognitive empathy (the ability to take the perspective of the other person). However, there were no differences between the two groups on emotional empathy (the capacity to feel concern for someone you think is in distress). This suggests that people diagnosed with Asperger's have a comparable amount of concern for the distress of others as do people without that diagnosis.[5] Whatever their brain activity, the environment in which children are brought up will make a difference to whether empathy is nurtured or suppressed.

An unempathic environment

One of the things that first got me interested in empathy was reading in the UK news about James Bulger, a Merseyside toddler who was abducted, tortured, and killed by two ten-year-old boys (Robert Thompson and Jon Venables). Clearly the boys hadn't developed the capacity to empathize with their victim. What could have been missing in their characters and upbringing?

Robert Thompson was the main instigator. His father had left the family five years previously, one week before the family home was burned down. His mother, Ann Thompson, was a heavy drinker who found it difficult to control her seven children. Case notes held by the National Society for the Prevention of Cruelty to Children (NSPCC) described the family as 'appalling'. The children bit, hammered, battered, and tortured each other. Incidents in the report include the third child, Philip, threatening his older brother Ian with a knife. Ian asked to be taken into foster care. When he was returned to his family, he attempted suicide with painkillers. Ann and Philip had also attempted suicide.[6]

A 1995 Home Office report, commissioned partly in response to fears raised by the Bulger case, made a link between a violent home background and youth offending. It found a pathway from a violent home background, to being an offender, to be being more likely to prefer violent films and violent actors. In addition, distorted perceptions about violent behaviour, poor empathy for others, and what the report called 'low moral development' all increased the likelihood of violent behaviour and violent film preferences.[7]

The healthy development of empathy

In 2008 the Dalai Lama participated in a conference on the scientific basis of compassion with a panel of expert child psychologists, psychotherapists, and neuroscientists.[8] In stark contrast to the previous story, the panel traced the healthy development of empathy in children.

As we saw in Chapter 1, body-mapping begins at birth: a new-born human baby will stick out its tongue in response to an adult doing so. For apes and monkeys it is the same: they will mimic a researcher slowly opening and closing his mouth. Imitation is the tendency to adopt the situation, emotions, and behaviour of those you are close to. It also starts early in children – they will often imitate the walk, dress, and speech of the parent of the same sex. Think of a baby girl holding a doll in her arms like her mother, or pushing it around in a buggy!

Empathy proper seems to emerge between the first and the third year.[9] In some studies, a researcher who is not known to the child uses a hammer to tap a nail into a wall. If the researcher taps the nail and then says, 'Ouch! Oh, I hurt my finger', the child will look up at the adult and begin to be concerned about the hurt finger. Some three-year-olds will even pick up their own teddy bear, walk over, and offer it to the stranger to comfort them. So we can be pretty sure that a deep sense of compassion and caring for others emerges between the first and third year.[10]

The Dalai Lama was asked whether he thought that humans are born with empathy and compassion, or whether these qualities need cultivation by the family – or both. He replied that humans are social animals, and that we are dependent for survival on the care of others. There must be an emotional (mental) factor that brings about this care. This emotional factor could be on the child's side or the mother's side or both. In practice, it seems to be both. As soon as a child or animal is born, it immediately tries to rely on its mother or caregiver. Despite the difficulties of giving birth, the mother is usually enthusiastic to care for her baby. The baby's body needs care for survival. The factors that bring about this care are not intellectual but biological.

By way of contrast, turtle mothers lay their eggs and leave. Turtle mothers are unlikely to have a capacity for affection. There is no need for maternal care for their offspring to survive. Turtles don't need affection and compassion. But our survival as humans is entirely dependent on our caregiver's care. So the Dalai Lama concluded that compassion is natural. Some kind of emotion is necessary to bring mother and child together. From this perspective, care in humans is biological and innate.

Children see the world through the lens of *how their parents treat them*. Children look for messages concerning these questions: who are they? Are they deserving of love? They cry as an expression of a need to know that mummy is there for them. Children who have at least one relationship that gives them a sense of hope and a sense of being cherished develop better and can survive extremely adverse circumstances.

Secure attachment and empathy

Another panellist that day was Dr Dan Siegel, psychotherapist and neuroscientist. He has also researched the link between mindfulness and empathy.[11] Siegel co-wrote a book called *Parenting from the Inside Out* based on extensive research into attachment theory.[12] Attachment theory explores how children form secure attachments to their parents and/or caregivers. The theory suggests that you are born with the longing to seek out one or more wiser/stronger figures. This/these figure(s) provide a safe haven for comfort, security, and meeting basic needs.[13]

Extensive worldwide research suggests that there are four basic attachment styles. These begin in early childhood as a result of relationship(s) with the primary caregiver(s), and persist in later life. There are three organized attachment styles: secure attachment, avoidant attachment, and anxious attachment. The fourth style is disorganized attachment.

Only one of these attachment styles is secure: the first. But what does it mean to be securely attached? A child who is securely attached is easy to soothe, confident, expects to be helped, has a positive sense of self and others, internalizes their caregiver as a source of comfort, and refers internally to her/him to feel safe while seeking stimulation elsewhere. We're all happiest when life is organized as a series of excursions from the secure base provided by our attachment figures.[14]

But Dan Siegel had a question for the audience: what is the best predictor on the *caregiver's* side of the attachment style of a child? What quality of the caregiver influences most strongly whether the child is securely attached or not? Could it be how communicative you are? Could it be how much you love the child? Or a strong moral sense? Siegel had a surprising answer: the best predictor of how children turn out is how well their caregiver has *made sense of their own lives*. For caregivers, this means getting in touch with feelings that are left over from their childhood. It means mourning losses if necessary, and understanding lessons. When you have done this, you are free to tune in to your child.

This type of attunement involves noticing verbal and non-verbal signals and responding in ways that say, 'I have seen you.' It gives the child the experience of 'feeling felt'. It needn't take more time. It could simply be pausing and reflecting: what is in your child's inner world? This supports the development of empathy and compassion in the child. It is profoundly important for a child's well-being in many ways.[15]

We can be securely attached either by temperament or from having received consistently empathic care in childhood. The effects continue through to adulthood. Adults who are securely attached are more likely to act with empathy, compassion, and responsive, altruistic behaviours.[16] Boosting attachment security increases compassion and helping.[17] Securely attached people are also known to show greater tolerance of out-groups, have a higher sense of self-worth, show less reactivity to criticism, and be more open-minded and flexible in their thinking.[18]

However, if you're not securely attached by temperament or upbringing, all is not lost! As an adult, your brain is still malleable. As adults we can develop secure attachment through sustained relationships with emotionally healthy, empathic mentors, teachers, friends, and partners. There is also evidence that mindfulness practices such as meditation and yoga can provide similar psychological and neurological benefits as secure attachment.[19]

The point is clear. As Dr Stanley Greenspan, clinical professor of psychiatry and paediatrics at George Washington University School of Medicine wrote in his book *Great Kids*, 'Empathize with your child. Empathy comes from being empathized with.'[20] This view is echoed by neuroscience. The ability to empathize develops in children through imitative interactions with their attuned caregivers.[21]

Tuning in to your children encourages them to develop empathy. You can also encourage your children to reflect on the consequences of their actions. As we saw in Chapter 2, the Buddha came across a gang of boys tormenting a crow with a broken wing.[22] The Buddha didn't tell them to stop, and didn't make judgements of them. Instead, he asked them to compare their own experience with that of the crow. Does it hurt when you get hit? When they appreciated that the crow probably felt pain in the same way as them, they put down their sticks and went to find a different game. It's unlikely that Robert Thompson received attuned caregiving, or was encouraged to reflect on the consequences of his actions.

Attachment research has shown the link between childhood care and the development of empathy and compassion. Adverse childhood care is linked to later violence. The most robust evidence comes from a wide-ranging study of 17,337 American adults. They were questioned about eight adverse childhood experiences (ACEs): emotional abuse; physical abuse; contact sexual abuse; exposure to alcohol or other substance abuse; mental illness; violent treatment of mother or step-mother; criminal behaviour in the household; parental separation or divorce. These ACEs served as a measure of *cumulative* childhood stress. This stress led to impaired brain and physical development and resulted in long-term behavioural, health, and social problems. The more ACEs in childhood, the greater the risk faced by adults of emotional, bodily, memory, and sexual dysfunction, substance abuse, poor anger-control, and intimate partner violence. To give an idea of the power of these ACEs, if you score six or more, it could reduce your life expectancy by up to two decades.[23]

We all want to make the world safer for the future. Can we understand more deeply what motivated Robert Thompson and Jon Venables? They chose a younger boy to lead away. The grainy CCTV images show the smaller boy walking out of the shopping mall hand in hand between the two older boys. It's every parent's worst nightmare. The fact that they were hand in hand suggests that the older boys had won James' trust. They probably had to work hard to do this.

Why did the older boys pick a younger boy as their 'victim'? Did they want to inflict the same kind of pain on another boy as they had experienced at the hands of people around them? By inflicting pain, did they find some relief for their own pain? Some satisfaction of knowing that another person is hurting? Some sense of being understood?

Notice your responses. Are you feeling horrified and fearful? Do you want children to be safe? Are you enraged because of the deep fear and pain that parents go through in relation to their children's safety? Do you want some kind of balance for the pain that James Bulger and his parents endured? Whatever your response, you are creating the future world with it.

One way to make a safer world is to learn how to empathize with children, even when there are things at stake. Sarah is mother to Josh, her four-year-old son. They live in a country where car seat belts are a legal requirement.

 Empathy exercise

- Purpose of this activity: to connect with a child's feelings and needs (and his mother's!)
- Tools: a notepad or journal and a pencil
- Time: 5–10 minutes

For each of the sentences in italics, try to sense the feelings and needs underneath. If you want, you can compare your guesses with mine at the end. If you notice judgements coming up in your mind, see if you can connect with the needs behind them, and then redirect your attention to the speaker's feelings and needs.

Sarah (anxiously remembering the conflicts on the last few car journeys): *Josh, we've got to put the seat belt on you now.*

Josh (shouting): *No!!!*

Sarah: We have to.

Josh: No! I don't like it!

Sarah: *The policeman will tell mummy off.*

Josh (wriggling): I don't care! *It's too tight.*

Sarah puts the seat belt on Josh by force, gets in the driver's seat, and sets off. *Josh cries and screams for the next 20 minutes.* When they arrive, *Sarah is angry and exhausted.* She lets Josh out of the car. *He runs into the garden and won't come into the house for dinner.*

Make a note of your own guesses about what is important to each speaker. Then, if you like, compare them with my guesses below.

My guesses

Josh, we've got to put the seat belt on you now. Sarah wants to protect Josh. At the same time, she is anxious and longing for ease.

No!!! Josh is angry and wants to make his own choices (need for autonomy).

The policeman will tell mummy off. Sarah wants peace of mind: freedom from worrying about Josh's safety and freedom from fear of legal punishment.

It's too tight. Josh also wants to be comfortable.

Sarah puts the seat belt on Josh by force. She is feeling hopeless about how to protect herself and Josh, other than putting the seat belt on Josh against his will.

Josh cries and screams for the next 20 minutes. Josh feels hurt and angry because he wants to be taken into account.

Sarah is angry and exhausted. Sarah is longing for ease and peace of mind.

He runs into the garden and won't come into the house for dinner. Josh needs some space to reconnect with his freedom. He needs to mourn the loss of connection and not being taken into account. He also wants understanding for his pain. He hopes that, when he cuts the connection with his mother, she will experience the pain of disconnection, thereby creating some balance and giving him understanding for his pain.

How did you get on? Did you hear the thoughts or the underlying feelings and needs? Make a note of it. Could you rewrite the conversation so that Sarah fully empathizes with Josh's needs *before* putting the seat belt on him?

A human being is part of the whole world, called by us 'Universe', a part limited in time and space. He experiences himself, his thoughts and feelings as something separate from the rest – a kind of optical delusion of his consciousness. This delusion is a kind of prison for us, restricting us to our personal desires and to affection for a few persons nearest to us. Our task must be to free ourselves from this prison by widening our circle of compassion to embrace all living creatures and the whole of nature in its beauty. Nobody is able to achieve this completely, but the striving for such achievement is in itself a part of the liberation, and a foundation for inner security.

– Albert Einstein[1]

Chapter fourteen

....

Empathy and compassion

As we've seen, empathy can be developed by directing our attention over time. There may even be a progressive path to empathy: starting with bodily awareness to provide a basis for mindfulness; cultivating mindfulness to provide a basis for self-empathy; cultivating self-empathy to provide a basis for empathy for others; and finally cultivating empathy for others to provide a basis for ethics and compassion for all.

Bodily awareness

The Buddha made mindfulness of the body the first of the four foundations of mindfulness. He emphasized that he was talking about awareness of the body in very simple terms: being aware of the body *as a body*. How are you breathing? What is your posture? Are you walking, standing, sitting, or lying down? Rather than thinking about your experience of your body, actually feeling the sensations associated with breathing, standing, sitting, or lying down.[2]

What helps? Anything that takes your attention from your thoughts to the internal state of your body. It might seem challenging if you spend your days thinking! One of the best ways to practise awareness of the internal sensations of the body is mindfulness meditation. Try a Mindfulness of Breathing meditation practice. This encourages you to focus on the sensations of breathing. All the while you're paying attention to your breathing, your attention is in your body rather than your head. If you do it daily for a few months, you'll gradually get more in touch with your internal sensations. You'll begin to notice changes in your breathing. Shortening or tightening

....

of the breath will alert you to changes in what you're feeling. Another type of mindfulness meditation is the body scan. Slowly bringing your attention to each part of your body in turn can bring a peace and stillness to your body and mind. Here's an exercise specifically for developing mindfulness of body, breath, and feelings.

  Exercise: awareness of body, breath, and feelings

- Purpose of this activity: to help you develop mindfulness of your body, breath, and feelings
- Tools: somewhere to sit quietly and comfortably, and a notepad or journal and a pencil (optional)
- Time: 15 minutes

Find a space where you can sit comfortably. If you meditate, you could include this exercise in your regular session.

Bring attention to your body. You could start with your toes and slowly work your way up the back of your body to your shoulders. Then down your arms to your hands (notice the sensations in your hands). Then switch to your belly, and your lower back again. Then follow your spine up to the neck and head. Then trickle your attention down the front of your body past your forehead to your eyes, nose, mouth, chin, and throat, until you reach your chest, with your heart and lungs.

Centre your attention in your chest. Notice the sensations associated with your breathing. Do you feel your chest rise and fall rhythmically with each breath? Do you feel your diaphragm moving? Can you feel the breath in your belly? Follow the rhythmic sensations of your breathing for several minutes.

When you're ready, bring your attention to what you're feeling at the moment. Start by checking in your heart, or around your heart, then lower down in your solar plexus or stomach and higher up in your throat or even head. See if you can notice where you feel this feeling in your body, and what it feels like (dull, dead, heavy, tight, tense, rising up, light, tingly, warm, relieving, cool, etc.).

After 10 minutes or so, drop the exercise and sit quietly, absorbing whatever has happened. If it helps, you might like to make a note of:

I'll Meet You There

- your recollection of the exercise;
- how you feel now;
- what touched you, doing the exercise – what did you learn from it?

Apart from meditation, any kind of mindful movement will help develop bodily awareness. This includes yoga, Pilates, sports like walking and swimming, martial arts, Alexander Technique, and dancing.

I maintain a daily practice of meditation and qigong (a form of taiji), and try to go for a brisk walk in the afternoon. When I'm at my computer, I try to be aware of my posture and breathing. In this way I care for my body and support its vitality.

Suggestion: make a list of activities you enjoy that would increase awareness and health in your body. Pick at least one to do on a daily or weekly basis.

Mindfulness

Bodily awareness provides a basis of mindfulness. As we've already seen, mindfulness involves expanding the range of your awareness from your body to include your feelings, state of mind, and what you are paying attention to at any given moment.

What helps? Mindfulness strengthens your ability to pay attention. Any activity requiring concentration can develop this. However, as with bodily awareness, mindful meditation and mindful movement top the list. Meditation is probably the most direct method, as you pay close attention to attention (awareness) itself. Mindfulness, like empathy, is 'caught, not taught'. Living and working with mindful people is the easiest way to catch it. If this isn't an option for you, journaling and mindful discussion with friends will help you keep track of your thoughts.

Any of the exercises in this book will help develop mindfulness. However, you don't need to be sitting quietly to practise mindfulness. Here's a traditional practice called walking meditation.

Exercise: walking meditation

- Purpose of this activity: to help you develop mindfulness of your body, feelings, state of mind, and mental contents
- Tools: somewhere to walk quietly and comfortably, and a notepad or journal and a pencil (optional)
- Time: 15 minutes

Find a 'lane' where you can walk backwards and forwards. If you meditate, you could include this exercise in your regular session.

Start walking slower than you usually walk, while keeping your balance. Bring your attention to the contact of your feet on the floor, one foot then the other. Notice how your ankles bend and flex with each step. Notice how your calves, knees, and thighs work in concert to move you forwards. Feel the movement in your hips as you transfer the weight from one leg to the other and bring your leg forwards. Notice how your belly stays relatively still as you walk. Feel the column of your spine supporting your torso. Notice how your shoulders and arms naturally swing in time with the movement of your hips. Notice any tension in your neck. Feel the air brushing against your face.

Centre your attention in your chest. Notice the sensations associated with your breathing. Do you feel your chest rise and fall rhythmically with each breath? Do you feel your diaphragm moving? Can you feel the breath in your belly? Follow the rhythmic sensations of your breathing for several minutes as you walk.

As you walk, bring your attention to what you're feeling. Check around your heart, lower down in your solar plexus, and higher up in your throat or even your head. See if you can notice where you feel this feeling in your body, and what it feels like (dull, dead, heavy, tight, tense, rising up, light, tingly, warm, relieving, cool, etc.).

What is your general state of mind as you walk? Is it contracted or expansive, light or dark, pleasant or unpleasant?

What is your attention drawn to? What is 'on your mind'? Can you be aware of it as thoughts and still keep awareness of walking?

After 10 minutes or so, drop the exercise and sit quietly, absorbing whatever has happened. If it helps, you might like to make a note of:

- your recollection of the exercise;
- how you feel now;
- what touched you, doing the exercise – what did you learn from it?

Self-empathy

Mindfulness provides a basis for self-empathy. Self-empathy means sensing the feelings and needs that are alive in you right now. Self-compassion is self-empathy for suffering. So self-empathy and self-compassion can involve healing painful memories.

What helps? Giving yourself the space to reconnect with yourself. Anything that allows you to 'feel felt', whether by yourself or by others. There is one approach in particular that stands out: observing, investigating, and reflecting on your inner mental states. What does this? Introspection, therapy, and – you guessed it – meditation.

When you're in a really difficult situation, you may not have time to meditate. As alternatives, you could ask for empathy or take time out. If even these aren't options, you might take time in. Taking time in means getting in touch with whatever is out of balance inside you. It means doing some self-empathy. It means clarifying your inner world. It means centring and regaining control of yourself. If you have space to connect with yourself, you have space to connect with the people around you.

 Exercise: taking time in

- Purpose of this activity: to reconnect with yourself in a stressful situation
- Tools: none
- Time: 3 seconds to 15 minutes

- Notes: at first you'll probably need to take yourself out of the heated situation to do this exercise. After a while, though, you'll find that you can take time in without taking yourself out of the situation.

See if you can mindfully listen for your thoughts about the situation. What's the story you're telling yourself? Make a mental note of it.

What is specifically triggering you in this situation? Is it something that somebody else said or did? Is it their tone of voice? Is it something you did? Is it your own thoughts? Try and recall it exactly.

Sense what you're feeling as you recall the trigger. If it helps, you could look at the list of feelings in Appendix B. See if you can find where you feel this feeling in your body, and what it feels like: dull, dead, heavy, tight, tense, rising up, light, tingly, warm, relieving, cool, etc. Does this feeling have a colour or a sound or an image associated with it?

When you are fully in touch with your feeling, ask yourself, 'What am I longing for? What's the need behind or underneath this feeling?' If it helps, you could use the list of needs in Appendix A. Stay with this process until something shifts, the feeling changes in quality or changes into another feeling. This 'shift' is a sign that you are connecting with the need, your deeper motivation. When you notice that something has changed, that you have some space inside, check which need you are now in touch with. Do you really long for respect, or consideration, or care in communication?

When you are fully present with your need, check whether there is a specific next step that you want to take to meet it, e.g. empathizing with the other person, or expressing what's in your heart, or some other action.

Self-empathy can also take place over a longer period of weeks, months, or years. It can be facilitated by keeping a journal, perhaps each night before you go to bed, where you record painful triggers and the feelings and needs relating to them. In the same journal, you could practise celebrating met needs, even keeping a gratitude journal. The process can be supported by asking others to help you explore what is important to you.

Empathy for others

Self-empathy provides a basis for empathy for others. As you become increasingly aware of your own feelings and needs, you develop an increasing awareness of the feelings and needs of others. Empathy is simply a mindful awareness of others.

What helps? As with the previous steps, we need to engage in intense experiential learning. In order to bring about lasting changes in your brain and consciousness, you need to stimulate feelings as well as understanding.[3] You can use meditation again. Try any of the exercises in previous chapters that involve bringing other people to mind. Through repeatedly connecting with and imagining the experience of other people you can strengthen your ability to empathize.

In workshops you have the advantage of training with others. The workshop facilitator can model empathy skills by empathizing with participants. Participants can engage in role-play or semi-role-play situations where they can practise empathy skills in a safe learning environment. Right now, you could review Chapter 8 and do the exercises there. Through years of practice, you build up a more accurate 'map' of what might be going on for other people. You still make a guess though, rather than try to diagnose them! You could also look into undertaking ethical training principles, such as the ones described below, which will sensitize you to the life around you.

Self-empathy (self-compassion) is crucial to empathizing with others. When you are fully in empathy with yourself, there is a welling up of curiosity about others. There's nothing laboured or forced about it. So, if you're finding it difficult to empathize with someone, you can go back and reconnect with yourself.

What are you longing for? Generally you want connection with yourself *and* others. But sometimes you get stuck in the trap of telling yourself that you 'should' empathize. However, there can be a natural transition between self-empathy and empathy for others. That's how mediation works. You listen to people deeply, support them to self-empathize. After a while they realize that they've had enough empathy for the time being. Naturally and spontaneously they want to look over the wall and find out what has been going on for the other person.

Empathy and compassion

As explored in Chapter 10, empathy provides a basis for acting ethically and for compassion. Empathy comprises a sense of connection and a sense of imagination. A sense of connection enables you to see the life in other beings. A sense of imagination allows you to guess how they will experience your actions. On this basis, you are able to assess whether your actions will contribute to their well-being or not.

But what is compassion? According to Buddhism, compassion is an emotion, but one that involves reflection. It has a cognitive, reflective element. Some emotions, such as revulsion at the sight of blood, are basically instinctual. Others, such as fear of poverty, have a more developed cognitive component. Compassion is a combination of empathy and reason.[4]

What is the difference between empathy and compassion? Compassion is broader in its scope of application than empathy. By definition, compassion is unconditional: it is towards all sentient beings, at all times. This is in contrast to empathy, which is usually only directed towards people who are similar and familiar, for instance family, friends, and the groups you identify with.

Secondly, empathy is *a way* of embodying compassion. The Tree of Compassionate Connection in Chapter 4 makes clear that you have choices about how you embody compassion. You can (i) self-empathize, (ii) empathize with the other person, or (iii) honestly express what's in your heart. In the field of action, you can (iv) act practically to alleviate pain. All four are ways to personalize compassion and give it real traction.

Thirdly, compassion in its fullest sense is a spontaneous outpouring, which goes beyond the sense of self and other. In the Introduction, Rumi invited us to lie down in a field, beyond ideas of wrongdoing and rightdoing, where ideas, language, and even the concept of 'each other' don't make any sense.

Compassion is the active dimension of empathy. Empathy personalizes compassion and gives it traction. It is the aspect of compassion that reaches out to meet others where they are rather than where you would like them to be. You naturally extend your empathy to family, friends, and people you're close to. By contrast, 'unlimited' compassion extends even to your enemies – in fact to all sentient beings.

What helps? One way is to direct attention onto your existing feelings of empathy. This will expand those feelings and allow them to transform into love and compassion itself. My Buddhist teacher Sangharakshita was involved in the mass conversion of Indians to Buddhism. In the 1980s he addressed a crowd of thousands in Mumbai:

I believe that it is possible for any human being to communicate with any other human being, to feel for any other human being, to be friends with any other human being. This is what I truly and deeply believe. This belief is part of my own experience. It is part of my life. I cannot live without this belief, and I would rather die than give it up.[5]

'Feeling for' any other human being is a way of describing how empathy can expand into compassion. You can even extend your imaginative empathy to the natural world, and a sense of solidarity with all life. This is the true basis of ethics and compassion.

To pick up the thread of mindfulness, empathy is an *external* aspect of mindfulness. It's mindfulness of others. So another way to develop empathy is simply to develop mindfulness in general.

Another way to cultivate compassion is simply to act on your compassionate impulses. By doing this, you strengthen them and increase the likelihood that you will act on them again in the future. Marshall Rosenberg regarded acting compassionately as the best game in town. Contributing to life in this way was the most fun he'd ever had.

Where to start? Perhaps with the golden rule: do unto others as you would be done by. However, this might seem too vague to guide your actions. What about the ethics of empathy expressed by the Buddha? Could you be guided by his empathic understanding? The Buddha offered five training principles, or precepts, related to non-violence, property, sexual ethics, speech, and cultivating mindfulness.

The first training principle is non-violence, or love, and is the cornerstone of Buddhist ethics. Its primary expression is to abstain from taking life. However, it's not just about avoiding harm, it's also about acting with loving-kindness in order to purify your body, heart, and mind. You can generate clear guidelines for action from this principle. When people start practising it, they commonly try to reduce animal suffering by becoming vegetarian or vegan.

The second training principle relates to property and resources of all kinds. Abstaining from taking what is 'not given' means not stealing others' property. It also means being generous with what you have in an open-handed way. This is another way to purify your body, heart, and mind. In practice, this means clarifying what belongs to you and what doesn't, and checking out if you're not sure. It also means giving your resources freely, according to need.

The third training principle relates to sex: avoiding sexual misconduct. This means bringing an ethical perspective into the partly concealed world of sexual activity. Traditionally, examples of sexual misconduct are things like rape and adultery. However, it also includes bringing 'power over' into the sexual arena, so any kind of coercion. On the positive side, you can practise stillness, simplicity, and contentment in all areas of your life, not just in relation to sex. For instance, you could simplify your life, reducing input and consumption of resources of all kinds. As before, this will have the effect of purifying your body, heart, and mind.

The fourth training principle concerns communication. This means communicating truthfully on all levels. Avoid saying what you know to be untrue. Clarify the 'facts' of the matter, and know yourself deeply enough to be able to express yourself. Speak and listen in a way that is kindly, helpful, and harmonious. People who take up this precept typically pay greater attention to how accurately they report events, including other people's words, and notice more quickly when they have been inaccurate. Gradually they learn how to speak and listen in more compassionate, skilful ways that purify their speech.

The fifth training principle concerns developing mindfulness or awareness. It encourages you to avoid alcohol and drugs that cloud your mind. On the positive side, you can develop clear and radiant mindfulness. People who take up this practice typically reduce or stop taking intoxicants and take up meditation. In time, this will purify your mind.

Over the long term, reflection and rehearsal can be just as powerful as acting. As with the previous steps in a path to empathy, meditation can play an important part. Any loving-kindness or compassion meditation will help you reflect and rehearse. Try this one, below.

Exercise: empathy and loving-kindness

- Purpose of this activity: to explore empathy as a doorway to increasing loving-kindness
- Tools: somewhere to sit quietly and comfortably, and a notepad or journal and a pencil (optional)
- Time: 25 minutes

In the first stage, connect with yourself. What are you feeling in your body? And what's behind or underneath this feeling? What would give you a sense of wholeness and completeness? Do you need to love and be loved? Could it be connection, to be seen, or honesty? Perhaps compassion, ease, meaning, or purpose? Whatever it is, stay with this quality for a moment.

Notice that, when you get in touch with what you're longing for, the feeling changes in some way. Take this as a sign that you're in touch with what would give you a sense of wholeness. Imagine taking a step that would bring this life-enriching quality more fully into your life. It could be an action, or taking yourself somewhere where this quality is more present for you, even in a small way.

In the second stage, bring to mind a close friend, someone you feel warmly towards. Recall a time with them when you really enjoyed their company. Notice how that enriched both your lives. Get a sense of what makes your friend's life richer, more whole and complete. Do they need love? Or perhaps meaning? Or challenge? Perhaps they appreciate honesty. Maybe they love to play and be creative? If you get stuck, come back to what you're feeling and what's important to you for a moment. Then go back to your close friend.

Rejoice in what your close friend loves in their life. Imagine taking a step that would bring more of what they love into their life ... perhaps giving them a present, or doing something they enjoy with them.

In the third stage, bring to mind someone you feel neutral towards. It could be someone like the postman, whom you see regularly, but don't have a particular connection with. Imagine what's important to this person, what they love in life, what they find enriching. Perhaps they value the love and care of their family? Perhaps they get a sense of purpose from their work? Perhaps they enjoy contributing to life? Perhaps they love going on holiday, or have a passion for playing music? Get a sense of whatever enriches their life.

If you're finding it difficult, as before, check back with yourself. Notice what you're feeling and what's important to you. When you're ready, go back to the neutral person, and imagine taking a small step that would enrich their life ... perhaps making them a gift, or helping them in some way. Even just smiling at them.

In the fourth stage, bring to mind someone you find difficult, someone you have a conflict or disagreement with, or someone you tend to avoid. Notice how you feel as you bring them to mind, and what you're longing for. Do you want to be seen for who you are? Or do you need protection and security? Or a sense of connection?

Explore what this person might be longing for in their life, what they might be holding in their heart. Perhaps they are longing for love? Perhaps they long for a sense of purpose, or peace of mind? Perhaps they are missing a sense of connection, or cooperation? Get a sense of whatever would enrich their life.

If you're finding it difficult, come back to yourself, acknowledging what's in your own heart, what you might be feeling and needing at the moment. And, when you're ready, go back to the person that you find difficult. Try to get a sense of what's important to them, without necessarily agreeing with their world view or the way they go about doing things. Even cherishing them as a human being, regardless of your difficulties. And, if you can stretch to it, imagine taking a step towards them, towards enriching their life. Perhaps picking up the phone and calling them. Perhaps acknowledging any difficulties they have to them. Perhaps doing something with them that they enjoy, appreciate, or find fun.

In the fifth stage, bring to mind the people from the first four stages: yourself, your close friend, the neutral person, and the person you find difficult. Explore whatever enriches all your lives. Do you all need love and security? Do you value honesty? Are you longing for meaning and growth? Hold these life-enriching qualities in your heart. Imagine taking a step that enriches all your lives ... perhaps meeting with them, or offering them a drink, or smiling at each one in turn.

Staying connected with whatever enriches life, expand your attention to include the people in your building, the people in your street, your area. Spread out to include the people and animals in your state, country, continent, and hemisphere. Expand your awareness to include the whole earth, with its people and animals. Reaffirm your interconnectedness with humanity, with animal life, with the earth and the whole universe.

After 20 minutes, drop the exercise and take a few minutes to review:

- What touched you?
- What did you learn from this exercise?

If we could read the secret history of our enemies, we should find in each man's life sorrow and suffering enough to disarm all hostility.

– Henry Wadsworth Longfellow[1]

Conclusion

I'd like to finish with a challenge. By its very nature, compassion extends to our enemies, even to people we call 'terrorists'. But how practical is this? Is it even wise to try to empathize with 'terrorists'? What about the people who carried out the 9/11 attacks in the USA, or the 7 July 2005 bombings in London? Won't empathizing with them just encourage them, giving them the oxygen of publicity?

Let's stop for a moment and review. What are the human needs on both sides? As we've already found, exploring the needs of people in conflict makes it more likely that everyone's needs will be met. Let's look a little closer at some of the individuals on both 'sides' of those 7 July bombings in London.

Suppose you're a Londoner. Do you want to feel safe walking down the street or taking the Tube? Do you want to trust that people who have grievances with you or your government will try to resolve them by diplomatic means? Would you like the clarity and awareness that actions have consequences? Would you like understanding that bombs targeting civilians bring a depth of fear and pain that is hard to imagine? And that bombing civilians decreases the likelihood of the 'terrorists' being heard and their claims being recognized?

Now let's look at the 'terrorists' who carried out the attacks in London. Is it possible even to know their motivations? A little research reveals a number of final messages left by them. Here's a quote from a videotape aired by Al Jazeera TV station after the 7 July 2005 bombings in London. It's from one of the men who carried out the attacks, and died doing so. His name is Mohammad Sidique Khan:

> I and thousands like me are forsaking everything for
> what we believe. Our drive and motivation doesn't

come from tangible commodities that this world has to offer. Our religion is Islam, obedience to the one true God and following the footsteps of the final prophet messenger. Your democratically elected governments continuously perpetuate atrocities against my people all over the world. And your support of them makes you directly responsible, just as I am directly responsible for protecting and avenging my Muslim brothers and sisters. Until we feel security you will be our targets, and until you stop the bombing, gassing, imprisonment, and torture of my people we will not stop this fight. We are at war and I am a soldier. Now you too will taste the reality of this situation.[2]

Do you have the strength to empathize with this man? Does it even seem wise to do so? A relative of mine was in one of the three underground trains that was bombed that July morning. She was travelling to the café-bar where she worked as a manager. Her seat was next to a glass partition. When the bomb went off in the crowded carriage, the glass impacted her face.

It could have been me. On the morning of the attack, Mohammad Sidique Khan and his colleagues fanned out from King's Cross station. For twelve years, I lived in Cambridge and went down to London regularly for work and to visit my parents in Croydon. King's Cross is the main terminal for Cambridge trains.

I notice that I really do need some self-empathy. I can feel a tightening in my guts as I read Mohammad Sidique Khan's statement. I feel fearful. I realize that I want to be safe when I walk down the street or go on an underground train. I want my relatives to be safe too. I want people who have grievances with me or the UK government to resolve them by diplomatic means. I'd like awareness of the diffuse nature of responsibility in a democracy. I didn't vote for the party in government at that time, nor did I support their actions, for instance the 2003 invasion of Iraq. I'd like awareness that actions have consequences, and that bombing public places brings a depth of fear and pain that is hard to imagine. I'd like understanding that violence begets violence. I can see the truth of the Buddha's words, 'Not by hatred are hatreds ever pacified here in the world. They are pacified by love. This is the eternal law.'[3]

Now it's your turn. What self-empathy do you need to do? Remember that empathizing doesn't mean agreeing. Empathizing with someone's deeper motivations or needs doesn't mean that you agree with their world view or the means they use to meet their needs.

If you empathize with Mohammad Sidique Khan, it will only be because you want to meet your *own* need for connection. This is the ethics of empathy. Could you regain your connection with humanity, even if it means trying to understand something that appears incomprehensible? Do you have the strength to empathize with a person who is willing to kill and maim you, your family, and countryfolk, and end his life in the pursuit of his cause?

You can try to empathize. Was Mohammad Sidique Khan desperate, enraged, and passionate to uphold the dignity and autonomy of his religion and co-religionists? Was he so desperate about these needs being honoured that he was willing to use violence to try to meet them? Did he hope that his actions would be heard by the governments he saw as making it difficult for these needs to be met? Did he seek world attention for honouring and meeting these needs?

Looking more closely at Khan's statement, he wants understanding for the depth of his motivation. He is not seeking material benefit. He sees himself as responsible for protecting the religious community he was born into. He sees members of that community suffering as a result of the policies of certain Western governments. He'd like awareness of the depth of that suffering, and some kind of balance for it. He'd like understanding that those who elect governments are also responsible for their actions. He'd like Muslims worldwide to live safely and securely. He'd like understanding that he and others will continue to use violence until this comes about. He sees himself as a soldier fighting a war.

When you empathize like this, you're not agreeing with the strategies that Khan used. Nor are you agreeing with the world view that led to him taking these actions. However, you can still understand how he was trying to enrich his life and those of others. And through understanding you can regain a sense of connection with humanity.

That day, my relative was one of the lucky ones – she escaped with her life and her sight. She had a lot of surgery on the side of her face, and now, if she wears light make-up, you wouldn't notice. She seems to be at peace with herself. She never spoke about it afterwards, and she didn't go to the counselling that was offered or the public grieving, but she went through her own process and moved on. She learned to drive a car, provided by her company, so she doesn't have to use public transport. Now she is happily married.

Reconnecting with humanity, we come full circle to Śāntideva's *Bodhicaryāvatāra*. In order to cultivate *bodhicitta*, the desire for awakening for all beings, Śāntideva suggests that we reflect that 'All equally experience suffering and happiness.'[4] Other beings are just like us. If we help ourselves, there's no reason not to help beings like ourselves. Śāntideva also invites us to imagine ourselves as the other person. Can we put ourselves in their shoes, whether we regard them as inferior, equal, or superior? What are they thinking? What motivates them? What are they longing for and dreaming of? If we can do this with someone we see as inhuman, as a terrorist, could we do it with anyone? Could we do it with all life? In the following exercise, try expanding your empathy to include all beings.

  ### Exercise: a prayer for all beings

- Purpose of this activity: to explore the link between your own needs and the needs of all beings, in the context of prayer[5]
- Tools: somewhere to sit quietly and comfortably, and a notepad or journal and a pencil (optional)
- Time: 15 minutes

To help you arrive and become more mindfully present, scan through your body, follow your breathing for ten breaths, then bring your attention to your feelings.

When you are ready, get in touch with a need. For instance, it might be love and care. So you could say to yourself, 'I need love and care.' Connect with the life energy that this word embodies for you.

When you are in touch with the life energy that the word embodies, reflect: 'All beings need love and care.'

When you are ready, make a wish/prayer that includes yourself and all beings: 'May all beings be surrounded by love and care, both internally and externally, and may I be included among them.'

If another need comes to the surface, go through the same sequence for that need.

After 10 minutes, drop the reflection/prayer and take a few minutes to review:

- What touched you?
- What did you learn from this exercise?

Appendix A

Human needs

Survival

Air/water/light
Food
Health
Movement
Physical safety
Rest/sleep
Shelter
Touch

Protection

Order/structure
Safety
Security
Stability
Trusting

Well-being

Balance
Ease
Healing
Peace of mind
Vitality

To matter

Compassion
Consideration
Empathy
Respect
To be heard and seen
To be valued
Understanding

Regeneration

Celebration of life
Gratitude
Leisure
Mourning
Play

Transcendence

Beauty
Communion
Faith
Flow
Hope
Inspiration
Peace
Presence
Wholeness

Connection

Belonging
Closeness
Harmony
Love
Support
Tenderness
Warmth

Freedom

Autonomy
Choice
Control
Ease
Empowerment
Self-responsibility
Spontaneity

Honesty

Authenticity
Clarity
Integrity
Openness
Self-connection
Self-expression

Meaning

Challenge
Consciousness
Contributing to life
Creativity
Dignity
Growth
Learning
Mastery
Purpose
Understanding

Note: this list is provided only as a tool for study. No list is a substitute for finding your truth using the words that fit your experience.

This list builds on Marshall Rosenberg's original needs list (CNVC.org), with categories adapted from Manfred Max-Neef.[1]

Appendix B

....

List of feelings

Pleasant feelings

Curious

Alert
Amazed
Eager
Energized
Enthusiastic
Excited
Fascinated
Inspired
Interested
Intrigued
Playful

Happy

Confident
Delighted
Encouraged
Grateful
Hopeful
Joyful
Optimistic
Overjoyed
Proud
Relieved

Loving

Affectionate
Appreciative
Compassionate
Friendly
Moved
Nurtured
Open
Sensitive
Tender
Warm

Peaceful

Alive
Calm
Comfortable
Content
Fulfilled
Relaxed
Satisfied
Secure
Strong

Unpleasant feelings

Sad

Ashamed
Depressed
Despairing
Discouraged
Disheartened
Dismayed
Distressed
Guilty
Heavy
Hurt
Unhopeful

Angry

Aggravated
Annoyed
Appalled
Disgusted
Enraged
Furious
Indignant
Infuriated
Irritated
Jealous
Livid
Resentful

Frustrated

Agitated
Bored
Disappointed
Embarrassed
Exasperated
Helpless
Impatient
Tired
Upset

Surprised

Bewildered
Confused
Hesitant
Insecure
Puzzled
Shocked
Torn
Troubled

Afraid

Alarmed
Anxious
Fearful
Frightened
Nervous
Panicky
Scared
Terrified
Worried

....
Notes and references

Front matter

1 For more information, see www.CNVC.org.
2 In *Rumi: Selected Poems*, trans. C. Barks, Penguin, London 2004, p.36.

Chapter 1: The evolution of empathy

1 M.B. Rosenberg, *Nonviolent Communication: A Language of Life*, 2nd edn, PuddleDancer Press, Encinitas, CA 2003, p.151.
2 A version of this story appears in M.B. Rosenberg, *Speak Peace in a World of Conflict*, PuddleDancer Press, Encinitas, CA 2005, p.121.
3 F. de Waal, *The Age of Empathy*, Harmony Books, New York 2009.
4 F. de Waal, *The Age of Empathy*.
5 U. Dimberg, M. Thunberg, and K. Elmehed, 'Unconscious facial reactions to emotional facial expressions', *Psychological Science* 11 (2000), pp.86–9.
6 R.I.M. Dunbar and S. Shultz, 'Evolution in the social brain', *Science* 317:5843 (2007), pp.1344–7.

Chapter 2: The Buddha and Jesus

1 The wording in the catechism is 'to do unto others, as we would be done to ourselves'. See L. Vaux, *A Catechisme or Christian Doctrine* (1583), reprinted by The Chetham Society (Manchester 1885). It probably first appeared round 1567, but certainly in the reprint of 1583.
2 At a specialist symposium on this subject, most scholars favoured a date for the Buddha's death, or *Mahāparinibbāna*, within ten years of 400 BCE (before common era). See L.S. Cousins, 'The dating of the historical Buddha: a review article', *Journal of the Royal Asiatic Society* 6:1 (1996), pp.57–63.
3 For Siddhattha's royal parentage, see *Nālaka Sutta: To Nālaka* (*Sutta Nipāta* 3.11). See H. Saddhatissa, *The Sutta Nipāta*, Curzon,

....

London 1994. For another reference, see *The Mahāpadāna Sutta: The Great Discourse on the Lineage* (*Dīgha Nikāya* 14). See M. Walshe, *The Long Discourses of the Buddha: A Translation of the Dīgha Nikāya*, Wisdom Publications, Boston, MA 1995.

4 The four sights correspond to the 'messengers' who appear to the former Buddha Vipassī in *Dīgha Nikāya* 14. The account of the Buddha seeing the four sights occurs in the *Buddhavamsa* or *History of the Buddhas*, which is book 14 of the *Khuddaka Nikāya* (the fifth division of the Pali *Sutta Piṭaka*). The incident occurs in chapter 3: 'Seeing the four great omens'. See Tipitakadhara Mingun Sayadaw, 'Chronicle of Buddha Gotama', in *The Great Chronicle of Buddhas, volume two, part one*, trans. U Ko Lay and U Tin Lwin, 1994, available at http://realtruthlife.blogspot. co.uk/2011/08/maha-buddhavamsa-seeing-four-great.html#. WiLzvDdpG70, accessed on 5 December 2017. The story is enthusiastically retold by Aśvaghoṣa in his *Buddhacarita* or *Acts of the Buddha*, a Sanskrit biography of the Buddha. See Aśvaghoṣa, *Buddhacarita, or Acts of the Buddha*, trans. E.H. Johnston, Motilal Banarsidass, Delhi 1998.

5 *Sukhamala Sutta: Refinement* (*Aṅguttara Nikāya* 3.38). Available at www.accesstoinsight.org/tipitaka/an/an03/an03.038.than.html, accessed on 23 November 2017.

6 *The Ariyapariyesana Sutta* or *The Noble Search* (*Majjhima Nikāya* 26). See Ñanamoli Bhikkhu, *The Middle Length Discourses of the Buddha: A New Translation of the Majjhima Nikāya*, Wisdom Publications, Somerville, MA 1995.

7 In the original Pali, the phrase 'release their faith' is ambiguous. It could mean giving up (releasing) their previous faith, and it can also mean releasing (in the sense of developing) faith in the Buddha's teaching.

8 The story of the Buddha on retreat with the elephant is from the *Vinaya* (the section of the Pali texts concerned with monastic discipline), *Mahāvagga* 10.4. See Ñanamoli Bhikkhu, *The Life of the Buddha*, Buddhist Publication Society, Colombo 1992.

9 Rosenberg, *Nonviolent Communication*, p.1.

10 Sangharakshita, *The Buddha's Noble Eightfold Path*, 2nd edn, Windhorse Publications, Birmingham 2007, p.27, available under its earlier title of *Vision and Transformation* at https://www. sangharakshita.org/_books/Noble_Eightfold_Path.pdf, accessed on 23 November 2017. See the *Kumāraka Sutta: The Boys* (*Udāna* 5.4).

11 M.L. Hoffman, 'Discipline and internalization', *Developmental Psychology* 30:1 (1994), pp.26–8.

12 Manjusvara, 'A glimpse of the light', adapted from the 1989 Aid For India/Karuna Trust newsletter. Reprinted from *Golden Drum*

17 (1989), available at https://archive.li/HVPiP, accessed on 5 December 2017.

13 See above Chapter 2, note 1.

14 K. Armstrong, *Twelve Steps to a Compassionate Life*, Knopf, Toronto 2010.

15 G. Bernard Shaw, 'Maxims for revolutionists', in *Man and Superman*, Brentano's, New York 1905, p.227.

16 Luke 10:25–37.

17 Leviticus 19:18.

18 In Israel at that time, the Samaritans were regarded as an inferior race and treated unequally by the Jews. I'm grateful for Geoff Goodman's thoughts on the Good Samaritan and the woman caught in adultery; see G. Goodman, 'Feeling our way into empathy: Carl Rogers, Heinz Kohut, and Jesus', *Journal of Religion and Health* 30:3 (1991), pp.191–205.

19 This story appears at John 8:1–11.

20 P.B. Shelley, *A Defence of Poetry*, published posthumously in *Essays, Letters from Abroad, Translations and Fragments*, Edward Moxon, London 1840, p.17.

21 Sangharakshita, *The Ten Pillars of Buddhism*, 4th edn, Windhorse Publications, Birmingham 1996, p.56.

Chapter 3: The origins of the word 'empathy'

1 Evelyn Waugh, *Brideshead Revisited*, Penguin Classics, London 2000, p.31. Originally from the French proverb, 'Tout comprendre, c'est tout pardonner.'

2 J.B. Hunsdahl, 'Concerning *Einfühlung* (empathy): a concept analysis of its origin and early development', *Journal of the History of the Behavioral Sciences* 3:2 (1967), pp.180–91. See also G.W. Pigman, 'Freud and the history of empathy', *International Journal of Psychoanalysis* 76:2 (1995), pp.237–56.

3 There was an existing ancient Greek word *empatheia*, but this meant 'passion', or 'strong feeling', and doesn't seem to be related to the way Lipps used the word.

4 The word 'pity' is clearly used in the sense of 'empathy' by the eighteenth-century Dutch philosopher and satirist Bernard de Mandeville. See de Waal, *The Age of Empathy*.

5 'Empathy', in *American Heritage Dictionary of the English Language*, 4th new updated edn, Houghton Mifflin, Boston, MA 2009.

6 S.J. Haggbloom *et al.*, 'The 100 most eminent psychologists of the 20th century', *Review of General Psychology* 6:2 (2002), pp.139–52.

7 C.R. Rogers, 'The necessary and sufficient conditions of therapeutic personality change', *Journal of Consulting Psychology* 21 (1957), pp.95–103. See also C.R. Rogers, 'A theory of therapy, personality, and interpersonal relationships as developed in the

client-centered framework', in *Psychology: A Study of a Science*, vol.3: *Formulations of the Person and the Social Context*, ed. S. Koch, McGraw Hill, New York 1959, pp.184–256. Although this book is not primarily concerned with the therapist–client relationship, we can still make use of the research that Rogers and others have done in this setting.

8   G.T. Barrett-Lennard, 'Dimensions of therapist responses as causal factors in therapeutic change', *Psychological Monographs* 76:43 (1962), pp.1–36. Quoted in C.R. Rogers, *A Way of Being*, Houghton Mifflin, Boston, MA 1980, pp.143–4.

9   C.R. Rogers, 'Experiences in communication', a talk given to the California Institute of Technology, Pasadena, CA 1964.

10 A. Einstein, 'Religion and science', interview in *The New York Times Magazine*, 9 November 1930.

11 From the chapter on ethics from the third-century Bodhisattvabhūmi by Ācārya Asaṅgha. See M. Tatz, *Asanga's Chapter on Ethics, with the Commentary of Tsong-Kha-Pa: The Basic Path to Awakening, the Complete Bodhisattva*, trans. Mark Tatz, Edwin Mellen Press, New York 1989. Asaṅga is said to be one of the founders of the Yogacāra ('Mind only') school of Buddhism.

12 Buber was born in Germany in 1878, and deeply influenced by Søren Kierkegaard's existentialism and his native German/ Jewish culture.

13 E. Cashmore, *Rastaman: The Rastafarian Movement in England*, Allen & Unwin, London 1979.

14 S.L. Gaertner and J.F. Dovidio, 'The subtlety of white racism, arousal, and helping behaviour', *Journal of Personality and Social Psychology* 35 (1977), pp.691–707.

15 M.L. Hoffman, *Empathy and Moral Development: Implications for Caring and Justice*, Cambridge University Press, New York 2000.

16 C.D. Batson and J.L. Weeks, 'Mood effects of unsuccessful helping: another test of the empathy–altruism hypothesis', *Personality and Social Psychology Bulletin* 22 (1996), pp.148–57. See also C.D. Batson and L.L. Shaw, 'Evidence for altruism: toward a pluralism of prosocial motives', *Psychological Enquiry* 2 (1991), pp.107–22.

17 See, for example, D.M. Tice, E. Bratslavasky, and R.F. Baumeister, 'Emotional distress regulation takes precedence over impulse control: if you feel bad, do it!', *Journal of Personality and Social Psychology* 80:1 (2001), pp.53–67. See also C.D. Batson, S. Early, and G. Salvarini, 'Perspective taking: imagining how another feels versus imagining how you would feel', *Personality and Social Psychology Bulletin* 23:7 (1997), pp.751–8; E.J. Lawrence *et al.*, 'The role of "shared representations" in social perception and empathy: an fMRI study', *NeuroImage* 29 (2006), pp.1173–84; and C. Lamm, C.D. Batson, and J. Decety, 'The neural substrate

of human empathy: effects of perspective-taking and cognitive appraisal', *Journal of Cognitive Neuroscience* 19:1 (2007), pp.42–58.

18 S. Baron-Cohen, *Zero Degrees of Empathy: A New Theory of Human Cruelty*, Penguin, London 2011.

19 N.A. Arbuckle and W.A. Cunningham, 'Understanding everyday psychopathy: shared group identity leads to increased concern for others among undergraduates higher in psychopathy', *Social Cognition* 30:5 (2012), pp.564–83.

20 M.H. Davis, C. Luce, and S.J. Kraus, 'The heritability of characteristics associated with dispositional empathy', *Journal of Personality and Social Psychology* 62 (1994), pp.369–91. See also J.C. Loehlin and R.C. Nichols, *Heredity, Environment and Personality: A Study of 850 Sets of Twins*, University of Texas Press, Austin, TX 1976; and K.A. Matthews *et al.*, 'Principles in his nature which interest him in the fortune of others...': the heritability of empathic concern for others', *Journal of Personality and Social Psychology* 49 (1981), pp.237–47.

21 S.M. Rodrigues *et al.*, 'Oxcytocin receptor genetic variation relates to empathy and stress reactivity in humans', *PNAS* 106:50 (2009), pp.21437–41.

22 M. Schulte-Rüther *et al.*, 'Gender differences in brain networks supporting empathy', *NeuroImage* 42 (2008), pp.393–403.

23 See Schulte-Rüther *et al.*, 'Gender differences in brain networks supporting empathy'.

24 See M.H. Davis and H.A. Oathout, 'Maintenance of satisfaction in romantic relationships: empathy and relational competence', *Journal of Personality and Social Psychology* 53 (1987), pp.397–410. See also E.C.J. Long and D.W. Andrews, 'Perspective taking as a predictor of marital adjustment', *Journal of Personality and Social Psychology* 59 (1990), pp.126–31; and E.C.J. Long, 'Understanding the one you love: a longitudinal assessment of an empathy training program for couples in romantic relationships', *Family Relations* 48 (1999), pp.235–348.

25 J. Block-Lerner *et al.*, 'The case for mindfulness-based approaches in the cultivation of empathy: does nonjudgmental, present-moment awareness increase capacity for perspective-taking and empathic concern?', *Journal of Marital and Family Therapy* 33:4 (2007), pp.501–16.

26 A.M. Galinsky and F.L. Sonenstein, 'The association between developmental assets and sexual enjoyment among emerging adults', *Journal of Adolescent Health* 48:6 (2011), pp.610–15.

27 Sympathy is meant here in the sense of 'sharing of another's emotions' rather than in its broader sense as equivalent to compassion.

28 This quotation is usually attributed to Lilla Watson, but when interviewed she wasn't comfortable being credited for something

that had been born of a collective process. Her preference was that it be credited to 'Aboriginal activists group, Queensland, 1970s'. See https://en.wikipedia.org/wiki/Lilla_Watson, accessed on 5 December 2017.

29 B. Obama, *The Audacity of Hope*, Random House, New York 2006.

Chapter 4: Marshall and the Palestinians

1 Rosenberg, *Nonviolent Communication*, p.104.

2 A version of this story appears in Rosenberg, *Nonviolent Communication*, p.13.

3 H. Lifshitz, A. Kashtan, and M. Kashtan, 'Beacon for peace in the Promised Land: transforming Palestinian–Israeli relationships with Nonviolent Communication', in *Beyond Bullets and Bombs: Grassroots Peacebuilding Between Israelis and Palestinians*, ed. J. Kuriansky, Praeger, Westport, CT and London 2007, pp.111–18.

4 E. Marlow *et al.*, 'Nonviolent Communication training and empathy in male parolees', *Journal of Correctional Health Care* 18:1 (2012), pp.8–19.

5 J. Wachtel, *Toward Peace and Justice in Brazil: Dominic Barter and Restorative Circles* (2009), published online by the International Institute for Restorative Practices at www.iirp.edu/pdf/brazil.pdf, accessed on 5 December 2017.

6 This was in a 2006 conversation between Rosenberg and Jim Manske, NVC trainer and one-time coordinator of CNVC's Global Coordinating Circle, reported in the CNVC Certified Trainers Yahoo group, message #4199. In the conversation, Rosenberg credited Albert Ellis for beginning the process that resulted in 'needs' being a component of NVC early in his career. Ellis' work on 'I statements' stimulated him to clarify the cause of feelings. Rosenberg also stated that he didn't come across Abraham Maslow's work on needs until years later.

7 V.E. Frankl, *Man's Search for Meaning*, Rider, London 2004.

8 The others kinds of activity are sense-contact, attention, and perception. See Vasubandhu, *Abhidharmakośabhāṣyam of Vasubandhu*, trans. Leo M. Pruden, Asian Humanities Press, Berkeley, CA 1990 (translated into English from the French translation of Louis de La Vallée Poussin, *L'Abhidharmakośa de Vasubandhu*, Institut belge des hautes études chinoises, Brussels 1971).

9 Neuroscientists Jean Decety and P.L. Jackson come perilously close to this when they write 'Empathy accounts for the naturally occurring subjective experience of similarity between the feelings expressed by self and others without losing sight of whose feelings belong to whom. Empathy involves not only the affective experience of the other person's actual or inferred emotional

state but also some minimal recognition and understanding of another's emotional state.' See J. Decety and P.L. Jackson, 'The functional architecture of human empathy', *Behavioral and Cognitive Neuroscience Reviews* 3 (2004), pp.71–100 (p.71). See also J. Decety and M. Meyer, 'From emotion resonance to empathic understanding: a social developmental neuroscience account', *Development and Psychopathology* 20 (2008), pp.1053–80. Or here is a psychoanalytical definition from 1960: 'To empathize means to share, to experience the feelings of another person'; R.R. Greenson, 'Empathy and its vicissitudes', *International Journal of Psychoanalysis* 41 (1960), pp.418–24.

10 Psychologist Martin Hoffman avoids this knot of defining empathy as 'a match of feelings'. He defines empathy as 'an affective response more appropriate to another's situation than one's own'; see Hoffman, *Empathy and Moral Development*, p.4.

11 Rogers, 'A theory of therapy, personality, and interpersonal relationships as developed in the client-centered framework'. See also Rogers, 'The necessary and sufficient conditions of therapeutic personality change'.

Chapter 5: How not to empathize

1 Rosenberg, *Nonviolent Communication*, p.104.

2 H.A. Wilmer, 'The doctor–patient relationship and issues of pity, sympathy and empathy', *British Journal of Medical Psychology* 41 (1968), pp.243–8 (p.246).

3 The list first appears in Rosenberg, *Nonviolent Communication*, p.92. Rosenberg credits his friend Holley Humphrey for the list. Thanks also to NVC trainer Locana (Elizabeth English) for additions (personal communication). Her website: www. lifeatwork.co.uk.

4 Tice *et al.*, 'Emotional distress regulation takes precedence over impulse control: if you feel bad, do it!'

5 Lawrence *et al.*, 'The role of "shared representations" in social perception and empathy: an fMRI study'.

Chapter 6: Intention, presence, and focus

1 Rosenberg, *Nonviolent Communication*, p.127.

2 The headings build on the subject headings at 'How do you teach empathy?', found at http://www.radicalcompassion.com/ articles-and-practices/2005/7/31/how-do-you-teach-empathy. html, accessed on 5 December 2017.

3 M.B. Rosenberg, 'What is a definition of empathy?' (2003), audio-clip available at nvc-europe.org/SPIP/Empathy-and-surf, accessed on 23 November 2017.

4 Quoted in Rosenberg, *Nonviolent Communication*, p.91. From *The Way of Chuang Tzu* by Thomas Merton, Shambhala, Boston, MA 2004.
5 Thanks to NVC trainer Alan Seid for this image and clarity. His website: http://cascadiaworkshops.com.
6 M. Max-Neef, *From the Outside Looking In: Experiences in 'Barefoot Economics'*, Zed Books, London 1992. Originally published in 1982 (Dag Hammarskjöld Foundation, Uppsala).
7 Max-Neef, *From the Outside Looking In*. Max-Neef doesn't define or elaborate on this suggestion.
8 Thanks to NVC trainer Allan Rohlfs for expressing his concerns about needs lists. His website: https://allanrohlfs.com/.
9 A. Maslow, *Toward a Psychology of Being*, Van Nostrand, Princeton, NJ 1962.
10 K. Gibran, *The Prophet*, ed. Suheil Bushrui, Oneworld Publications, London 2012, p.17.

Chapter 7: Timing and sustaining empathy

1 Rosenberg, 'What is a definition of empathy?'
2 Rosenberg, *Nonviolent Communication*, p.104.
3 D. Hammarskjöld, *Markings*, Knopf, New York 1964, p.13.

Chapter 8: Empathy archery

1 R.N. Remen, *Kitchen Table Wisdom: Stories That Heal*, Riverhead Books, New York 2006, p.143–4.

Chapter 9: Empathy and mindfulness

1 H.D. Thoreau, *Walden, Volume One*, Houghton Mifflin, Boston, MA 1897, p.19.
2 M. Beitel, E. Ferrer, and J.J. Cecero, 'Psychological mindedness and awareness of self and others', *Journal of Clinical Psychology* 61 (2005), pp.739–50; M.B. Schure, J. Christopher, and S. Christopher, 'Mind–body medicine and the art of self-care: teaching mindfulness to counseling students through yoga, meditation, and qigong', *Journal of Counseling & Development* 86 (2008), pp.47–56; S.L. Shapiro, G.E. Schwartz, and G. Bonner, 'Effects of mindfulness-based stress reduction on medical and premedical students', *Journal of Behavioral Medicine* 21 (1998), pp.581–99; P.B. Greason and C.S. Cashwell, 'Mindfulness and counseling self-efficacy: the mediating role of attention and empathy', *Counselor Education and Supervision* 49 (2009), pp.2–19; M.S. Krasner *et al.*, 'Association of an educational program in

mindful communication with burnout, empathy, and attitudes among primary care physicians', *JAMA* 302:12 (2009), pp.1284–93.

3 Reported in Block-Lerner *et al.*, 'The case for mindfulness-based approaches in the cultivation of empathy'.

4 D.J. Siegel, *The Mindful Brain: Reflection and Attunement in the Cultivation of Well-Being*, W.W. Norton, New York 2007.

5 The simile comes in *Aṅguttara Nikāya* 4.107. See Nyanaponika Thera and Bhikkhu Bodhi, *Numerical Discourses of the Buddha: An Anthology of Suttas from the Anguttara Nikaya*, AltaMira Press, Lanham, MD 2000.

6 Subhuti, 'Mindfulness and the mind', *Madhyamavani* 8 (spring 2003).

7 *Parinibbāna Sutta: Total Unbinding* (*Samyutta Nikāya* 6.15).

8 *Majjhima Nikāya* 10. See Nyanaponika Thera, *The Heart of Buddhist Meditation: A Handbook of Mental Training based on the Buddha's Way of Mindfulness*, Rider and Company, London 1962.

9 Nyanaponika Thera, *The Heart of Buddhist Meditation*, p.58.

10 Buddhaghosa's *Visuddhimagga*, chapter 4, §49. See Buddhaghosa, *The Path of Purification: Visuddhimagga*, trans. Bhikkhu Ñāṇamoli, BPS Pariyatti Editions, Seattle, WA 1999.

11 K.E. Gerdes *et al.*, 'Teaching empathy: a framework rooted in social cognitive neuroscience and social justice', *Journal of Social Work Education* 47 (2011), pp.109–31. See also S.M. Erisman, K. Salters-Pedneault, and L. Roemer, 'Emotion regulation and mindfulness', poster presented at the annual convention of the Association for Advancement of Behavior Therapy, Washington, DC (17–20 November 2005); and Siegel, *The Mindful Brain*.

12 Discussed in Siegel, *The Mindful Brain*.

13 V.S. Ramachandran, who has been described as a latter-day Marco Polo of neuroscience by Richard Dawkins. See V.S. Ramachandran, 'Mirror neurones and imitation learning as the driving force behind "the great leap forward" in human evolution', available at https://www.edge.org/conversation/mirror-neurons-and-imitation-learning-as-the-driving-force-behind-the-great-leap-forward-in-human-evolution, accessed on 5 December 2017.

14 See V. Gallese *et al.*, 'Action recognition in the premotor cortex', *Brain* 119 (1996), pp.593–609. I feel torn about reporting this research, in the knowledge that the monkeys in question had electrodes implanted in their brains to measure the firing of specific neurones. I'm torn because I value and respect the lives of all sentient beings, including monkeys.

15 This story is apocryphal: in fact, there was no 'Aha!' moment. The initial findings were so implausible, given the researchers' understanding of the brain, that they were ignored. It was only years later, when the importance of 'mirror neurones' was

understood, that the researchers went back to their notes and found a variety of odd results, with no clear 'first instance'. See M. Iacoboni, *Mirroring People: The New Science of How We Connect with Others*, Farrar, Straus and Giroux, New York 2008.

16 V. Gallese, 'The roots of empathy: the shared manifold hypothesis and the neural basis of intersubjectivity', *Psychopathology* 36:4 (2003), pp.171–80. See also A.I. Goldman and C.S. Sripada, 'Simulationist models of face-based emotion recognition', *Cognition* 94 (2005), pp.193–213; C. Keysers and V. Gazzola, 'Towards a unifying neural theory of social cognition', *Progress in Brain Research* 156 (2006), pp.379–401; G. Rizzolatti, L. Fogassi, and V. Gallese, 'Neurophysiological mechanisms underlying the understanding and the imitation of action', *National Review of Neuroscience* 2 (2001), pp.661–70; and B. Wicker *et al.*, 'Both of us disgusted in My insula: the common neural basis of seeing and feeling disgust', *Neuron* 40 (2003), pp.655–64.

17 J.A.C.J. Bastiaansen, M. Thioux, and C. Keysers, 'Evidence for mirror systems in emotions', *Philosophical Transactions of the Royal Society of Biological Sciences* 364 (2009), pp.2391–404; Keysers and Gazzola, 'Towards a unifying neural theory of social cognition'; R.G. Benoit *et al.*, 'When I think about me and simulate you: medial rostral prefrontal cortex and self-referential processes', *NeuroImage* 50 (2010), pp.1340–9.

18 Gallese, 'The roots of empathy; Iacoboni, *Mirroring People*; M. Iacoboni *et al.*, 'Reafferent copies of imitated actions in the right superior temporal cortex', *Proceedings of the National Academy of Sciences* 98:24 (2001), pp.13995–9; M. Iacoboni *et al.*, 'Cortical mechanisms of human imitation', *Science* 286:5449 (1999), pp.2526–8; G. Rizzolatti and L. Craighero, 'The mirror neurone system', *Annual Review of Neuroscience* 27 (2004), pp.169–92; Rizzolatti *et al.*, 'Neurophysiological mechanisms underlying the understanding and the imitation of action'.

19 L. Carr *et al.*, 'Neural mechanisms of empathy in humans: a relay from neural systems for imitation to limbic areas', *Proceedings of the National Academy of Sciences* 100:9 (2003), pp.5497–502.

20 *Dhammapada*, verses 129–30. See *Dhammapada: The Way of Truth*, trans. Sangharakshita, Windhorse Publications, Birmingham 2001.

Chapter 10: The ethics of empathy

1 *Dhammapada*, verses 129–30. See also the probably earlier variant from *Sutta Nipāta* 704–5: 'comparing oneself to others in such terms as "Just as I am so are they, just as they are so am I", he should neither kill nor cause others to kill.' See Saddhatissa, *The*

Sutta Nipāta. Thanks to Stephen Batchelor for pointing out this additional reference.

2 M.R. Leary *et al.*, 'Self-compassion and reactions to unpleasant self-relevant events: the implications of treating oneself kindly', *Journal of Personality and Social Psychology* 92 (2007), pp.887–904.

3 The four noble truths are part of the 'Turning the wheel of the Dharma' sermon. See *Dhammacakkappavattana Sutta: Setting Rolling the Wheel of Truth* (*Sutta Nipāta* 56.11), trans. from the Pali by Ñanamoli Thera, available at http://www.accesstoinsight. org/tipitaka/sn/sn56/sn56.011.nymo.html, accessed on 23 November 2017.

4 See Dalai Lama, *Ancient Wisdom, Modern World: Ethics for a New Millennium*, Little, Brown, London 1999, pp.75–6.

5 *Mallikā Sutta* (*Samyutta Nikāya* 3.8), in M. Walshe, *Samyutta Nikāya: An Anthology*, Buddhist Publication Society, Kandy 1985.

6 *Dhammapada*, verses 129–30.

7 Sangharakshita, *The Rainbow Road*, Windhorse Publications, Birmingham 1997, p.355–6.

8 *Tuvaṭaka Sutta* (*The Way to Bliss, Sutta Nipāta* 4.14.918), in Saddhatissa, *The Sutta Nipāta*, p.107.

9 Subhuti, 'Re-imagining the Buddha' (2010), available at www. sangharakshita.org/pdfs/imagining-the-buddha.pdf, accessed on 23 November 2017, p.16.

10 Urgyen Sangharakshita, quoted in Subhuti, 'Re-imagining the Buddha', p.17.

11 O. Lyons, 'An Iroquois perspective', in *American Indian Environments: Ecological Issues in Native American History*, ed. C. Vecsey and R.W. Venables, Syracuse University Press, New York 1980, pp.171–4.

Chapter 11: The empathic Buddha

1 This description of the Buddha appears in the *Aṅguttara Nikāya* 1.13.1. The translation is by my friend Dharmachari Dhivan (personal communication with the author, December 2009).

2 The story features in the *Cūḷagosiṅga Sutta*, the shorter discourse in Gosinga. See Ñanamoli Bhikkhu, *The Middle Length Discourses of the Buddha*, no.31.

3 Ñanamoli Bhikkhu, *The Middle Length Discourses of the Buddha*, p.302.

4 *Kucchivikara-vatthu: The Monk with Dysentery* (*Mahāvagga* 8.26.1–8), available at http://www.accesstoinsight.org/tipitaka/vin/mv/ mv.08.26.01-08.than.html, accessed on 23 November 2017.

5 Matthew 25:35–40.

6 The story of the Buddha mediating between Śākyans and Koliyans is traditionally associated with the teaching given

in the *Attadaṇḍa Sutta* in the *Sutta Nipāta* 935–54 ('Fear results from resorting to violence – just look at how people quarrel and fight!'). Found in G.P. Malalasekera, *Dictionary of Pali Proper Names*, Luzac, London 1960, reprinted in 2003 (Asian Educational Services, New Delhi). Available at www.metta.lk/pali-utils/Pali-Proper-Names/rohini.htm, accessed on 23 November 2017. It is also associated with the fifth-century *Commentary to the Dhammapada*, found in *Buddhist Stories from the Dhammapada Commentary*, part 2, trans. from the Pali by E.W. Burlingame, selected and revised by Bhikkhu Khantipalo, *Wheel* 324, Buddhist Publication Society, Kandy 1985. There the story is associated with *Dhammapada* verses 197–9 ('Happy indeed we live, friendly amid the haters. Among men who hate we dwell free from hate'). The Rohini incident is retold and discussed in 'Buddhism, world peace and nuclear war', by Urgyen Sangharakshita, reprinted in Sangharakshita, *The Priceless Jewel*, Windhorse Publications, Birmingham 1993, available at https://www.sangharakshita.org/_books/The Priceless Jewel.pdf, accessed on 23 November 2017.

Chapter 12: The moon at the window

1 Śāntideva, *The Bodhicaryāvatāra: A Guide to the Buddhist Path to Awakening*, trans. Kate Crosby and Andrew Skilton, Windhorse Publications, Birmingham 2002, verse 10.55.

2 Śāntideva, *The Way of the Bodhisattva: A Translation of the Bodhicharyavatara*, trans. Padmakara Translation Group, rev. edn, Shambhala, Boston, MA 2008, p.47.

3 Śāntideva, *The Bodhicaryāvatāra*, verse 8:90.

4 Śāntideva, *The Bodhicaryāvatāra*, verse 8:94.

5 Śāntideva, *The Bodhicaryāvatāra*, verse 8:102.

6 Śāntideva, *The Bodhicaryāvatāra*, verse 8:120.

7 Śāntideva, *The Bodhicaryāvatāra*, verse 8:165.

8 *Mahā-Saccaka Sutta: The Longer Discourse to Saccaka* (*Majjhima Nikāya* 36), trans. from the Pali by Ṭhānissaro Bhikkhu, available at http://www.accesstoinsight.org/tipitaka/mn/mn.036.than.html, accessed on 23 November 2017.

9 Sangharakshita, *Creative Symbols of Tantric Buddhism*, Windhorse Publications, Birmingham 2002.

10 Found in N. Senzaki and P. Reps, *Zen Flesh, Zen Bones*, Penguin, London 2000. It may well be based on Ryōkan's haiku:
The thief
Left it behind–
The moon at the window.

This haiku is found in J. Stevens, *One Robe, One Bowl: The Zen Poetry of Ryōkan*, Weatherhill, Boston, MA 2006, p.75.

Chapter 13: Empathy in children

1 R. Carver, 'Late fragment', in *A New Path to the Waterfall: Poems*, Atlantic Monthly Press, New York 1989, p.122.
2 Hoffman, *Empathy and Moral Development*.
3 C.L. Gillberg, 'The Emanuel Miller Memorial Lecture 1991: autism and autistic-like conditions – subclasses among disorders of empathy', *Journal of Child Psychology and Psychiatry and Allied Disciplines* 33 (1992), pp.813–42.
4 A. Klin *et al.*, 'Visual fixation patterns during viewing of naturalistic social situations as predictors of social competence in individuals with autism', *Archives of General Psychiatry* 59 (2002), pp.809–16. See also P.K. Kuhl *et al.*, 'Links between social and linguistic processing of speech in preschool children with autism: behavioural and electrophysiological measures', *Developmental Science* 8 (2005), F1–12.
5 I. Dziobek *et al.*, 'Dissociation of cognitive and emotional empathy in adults with Asperger syndrome using the Multifaceted Empathy Test (MET)', *Journal of Autism and Developmental Disorders* 38 (2008), pp.464–73.
6 See Blake Morrison's disturbing and moving account of the case in *As If*, Granta Publications, London 1998.
7 K. Browne and A. Pennell, 'The effects of video violence on young offenders', *Research Findings* 65, Home Office Research and Statistics Directorate, London 1998.
8 'A day of science and learning' with His Holiness the Dalai Lama, 11 April 2008, on the University of Washington campus. The panel included Dr Dan Siegel. Video footage of this event is available at http://uwtv.org/series/dalai-lama/, accessed on 5 December 2017.
9 Hoffman, *Empathy and Moral Development*.
10 Reported by Andrew Meltzoff, co-director, University of Washington Institute for Learning and Brain Sciences, at 'A day of science and learning' mentioned above. This is in Part 2 of the video footage of this event: http://uwtv.org/series/dalai-lama/, accessed on 5 December 2017.
11 Siegel, *The Mindful Brain*.
12 D.J. Siegel and M. Hartzell, *Parenting from the Inside Out: How a Deeper Self-Understanding Can Help You Raise Children Who Thrive*, Penguin, New York 2004.
13 J. Bowlby, *Attachment*, Basic Books, New York 1969.
14 J. Bowlby, *A Secure Base: Clinical Applications of Attachment Theory*, Routledge, London 1988, p.27.

15 Siegel, *The Mindful Brain*.

16 Remarkably, even when the researchers temporarily induced a state of 'secure attachment' in subjects who were not securely attached by disposition or childhood care, they found that these subjects responded with corresponding empathy, compassion, and responsive, altruistic behaviours. See O. Gillath, P.R. Shaver, and M. Mikulincer, 'An attachment-theoretical approach to compassion and altruism', in *Compassion: Conceptualizations, Research, and Use in Psychotherapy*, ed. P. Gilbert, Routledge, Hove and New York 2005, pp.121–47. See also M. Mikulincer and P.R. Shaver, 'Attachment security, compassion, and altruism', *Current Directions in Psychological Science* 14:1 (2005), pp.34–8.

17 M. Mikulincer *et al.*, 'Attachment, caregiving, and altruism: boosting attachment security increases compassion and helping', *Journal of Personality and Social Psychology* 89 (2005), pp.817–39.

18 Summarized by Mitch Hall in 'Roots of empathy and nonviolence in childhood: a presentation and dialogue', available with accompanying slides at http://cultureofempathy.com/Projects/Interviews/2010-12-08-AHIMSA/, accessed on 23 November 2017.

19 P.R. Shaver *et al.*, 'Social foundations of the capacity for mindfulness: an attachment perspective', *Psychological Inquiry* 18 (2007), pp.264–71.

20 S.I. Greenspan, *Great Kids: Helping Your Baby and Child Develop the Ten Essential Qualities for a Healthy, Happy Life*, Da Capo Press, Cambridge, MA 2007, p.43.

21 Iacoboni, *Mirroring People*, pp.133–5.

22 See above Chapter 2, note 10.

23 R.F. Anda *et al.*, 'The enduring effects of abuse and related adverse experiences in childhood: a convergence of evidence from neurobiology and epidemiology', *European Archives of Psychiatry and Clinical Neuroscience* 256 (2006), pp.174–86.

Chapter 14: Empathy and compassion

1 A. Einstein, letter of 1950, as quoted in *The New York Times* (29 March 1972) and *The New York Post* (28 November 1972).

2 *Majjhima Nikāya* 10. Found in Nyanaponika Thera, *The Heart of Buddhist Meditation*.

3 H.M. Schachter *et al.*, 'Effects of school-based interventions on mental health stigmatization: a systematic review', *Child and Adolescent Psychiatry and Mental Health* 2:18 (2008), pp.1–14 (p.8).

4 Dalai Lama, *Ancient Wisdom, Modern World*, pp.76–7.

5 Sangharakshita, *Dr Ambedkar's True Greatness*, Triratna Grantha Mala, Pune 1986, quoted in Sangharakshita, *Living with Kindness*, Windhorse Publications, Birmingham 2008, p.2.

Conclusion

1 Henry Wadsworth Longfellow, *Driftwood*, found in *The Prose Works of Henry Wadsworth Longfellow, Revised Edition, Volume 3*, Ticknor and Fields, Boston, MA 1866, pp.361–2.
2 Al Jazeera, 1 September 2005, available at http://english. aljazeera.net/, accessed on 23 November 2017.
3 *Dhammapada*, verse 5.
4 Śāntideva, *The Bodhicaryāvatāra*, verse 8:90.
5 Inspired by Bridget Belgrave. See B. Belgrave, 'Being in touch with your needs can become a prayer for all beings', available at http://www.liferesources.org.uk/needs-as-a-prayer.pdf, accessed on 23 November 2017.

Appendix A: Human needs

1 M. Max-Neef *et al.*, 'Human scale development: an option for the future', *Development Dialogue* 1 (1989), pp.5–80.

Index

Introductory Note

References such as '178–9' indicate (not necessarily continuous) discussion of a topic across a range of pages. Wherever possible in the case of topics with many references, these have either been divided into sub-topics or only the most significant discussions of the topic are listed. Because the entire work is about 'empathy', the use of this term (and certain others which occur constantly throughout the book) as an entry point has been restricted. Information will be found under the corresponding detailed topics.

beauty 17, 56, 119, 143, 147–8, 162
begging bowl 22, 110, 146
behaviour
  criminal 158
  social 10, 12–13
  violent 154
beings 19–22, 119, 121, 129, 141–3,
    145–6, 148–9, 180–1
  hell 143
  living 118, 123
  sentient 21, 123, 170
  social 115
  tormented 146
belief 68, 133, 171
Bhavacakra 143, 146
blame 6, 8, 27, 51, 72, 91–2, 95–6
blaming 27, 93
bodhi tree 19, 110
Bodhicaryāvatāra 141, 180
bodhicitta 141, 180
bodhisattvas 34, 141
bodily awareness 115–16, 163–5
body 79, 81, 86–7, 112, 115–16,
    129–31, 163–6, 171–3
body scan 164
bombings 177–8
bonding 11, 39, 41
borderline personality disorder 37–8
Brahma Sahampati 19–20
brahma vihāras 125
brain 12–13, 37–8, 91, 113–16, 157,
    168
brain-scan studies 37, 113
Brazil 54
breathing 90, 109, 111–12, 116,
    163–6, 180
Buber, Martin 35
Buddha, and Jesus 17–30
Buddhist perspective 1, 107
Buddhist tradition 21, 23, 34, 111,
    121
Bulger, James 154, 159
bystanders 36

capacity
  for empathy 14, 31, 37–41, 109,
    124, 143, 153–4
  to imagine 12, 27–8, 38
care 13, 15, 25, 34, 131, 137–8, 154–5,
    181
caregivers 133, 155–7

catechism 23
cetanā 55
charity 41–2
chest 29, 116, 164, 166
childhood 34, 115, 156–8
children 5, 11–13, 22–3, 50, 60, 146–7
  empathy in 1, 153–62
choice 35, 38, 55, 77–8, 83, 87, 91–2,
    113
civil rights movement 34
closeness 40–1, 91, 119, 138, 184
  intense 1
clothes 25, 43, 147–8
cognitive empathy 153
collective welfare 130–1
colluding 64, 70–1, 74
comfort 15, 119, 155–6
  physical 130
common humanity 4, 27, 34, 42–3
communication
  nonviolent, *see* Nonviolent
    Communication (NVC)
  sexual 40
community 5, 7, 130–1, 179
  dialogues 52
  empathic 129, 132–3
comparisons 27, 115, 118, 123
  empathic 123–4
  invidious 123–4
compassion 19–25, 119–20, 125, 149,
    154–5, 157–8, 162–3, 169–71
  and empathy 22, 163–75
  meditation 172
compassionate action 70, 143
compassionate awareness 122
compassionate connection 22, 57,
    59, 78, 120, 170
compassionate intention 119, 148
completeness 112, 173
conflict 5–6, 8, 22, 133, 135–6, 143,
    174, 177
  external 136
  resolution 10, 35
connectedness 35
connection 51–2, 56–8, 68–71, 77–8,
    89, 102–5, 119–21, 147–8
  before correction 65–6, 87
  compassionate 22, 57, 59, 78, 120,
    170
  empathic 70
  genius for 147–9

sense of 169, 174, 180
consciousness 32, 38, 49, 55, 112, 120, 162, 168
   states of 55, 131–2
   sympathetic 21
consoling 64, 67, 74
contact 60–1, 80, 104, 125, 158, 166
contagion, emotional 10–12
contents, mental 112, 166
continuous awareness 32
control 51, 89, 100, 109, 154, 167, 184
cooperation 32, 174
correction 68, 88
   connection before 65–6, 87
costs 25, 143
counselling 137, 180
craving 120
creation 34, 82
creativity 15, 29, 120
criticism 6, 8, 72, 77, 92, 96, 157
crowds 10, 12, 26–7, 33, 170
cruelty 37–8
culture 34, 40–1, 44–5, 81, 83, 98, 119, 133
cumulative childhood stress 158
curiosity 78, 110, 169

Dalai Lama 121, 141, 154–5
Darwinism 10
de Waal, Frans 10
death 18, 26, 123
   violent 52
depression 53, 109
despair 51, 126
Detroit 22
development 1, 20–1, 23, 33, 78, 129
   healthy 154
   physical 158
   spiritual 112, 147
Dhammapada 27
Dhardo Rimpoche 23
Dharma 19, 129
Dheisheh refugee camp 49
diagnoses 5, 38, 72, 96, 153, 169
diaphragm 164, 166
dignity 44, 61, 67, 72–3, 82, 91, 121, 134–6
disciples 112, 129–31, 141
discomfort 65, 68, 138
disconnections 41, 69, 160
disorganized attachment 156

disputes 5, 42, 130–1, 133–4
distraction 18, 67–8, 71–2, 99, 110
distress 13, 36–7, 42, 70, 153
   empathic 36–7, 70
   psychological 33
doctors 63–4, 71, 88
dolphins 12–13
dreams 23, 41, 43, 69, 103, 117, 124
drugs 88–9, 172

ease 20–1, 29, 32, 55, 120, 126, 160, 183–4
ecological awareness 131
Eden Project 57–8
education 32, 34–5, 72
   empathy before 65–6, 87
egotism 56, 119, 123–4
Einfühlung 31
Einstein, Albert 34, 113, 162
electrodes 11, 36
elephants 13, 20, 110
emergencies 36, 55, 90–1
emotional abuse 158
emotional arousal 13
emotional contagion 10–12
emotional empathy 153
emotions 10–11, 41, 77, 155, 170
empathic Buddha 129–39
empathic community 129, 132–3
empathic comparison 123–4
empathic distress 36–7, 70
empathic insights 122, 145–6
empathic understanding 143, 145–6, 171
empathy, *see also Introductory Note*
   active dimension of 125, 170
   archery 1, 95–108
   before education 65–6, 87
   capacity for 14, 31, 37–41, 109, 124, 143, 153–4
   in children 1, 153–62
   cognitive 153
   and compassion 22, 163–75
   development 42, 115
   emotional 153
   ethics 23–4, 119–28, 141, 143, 171, 179
   evolution 5–15
   exercises 14, 28, 43, 60, 116, 125, 137, 148
   first-aid 90–1

guessing 50, 101–2, 117
guides 78, 81, 104, 141, 171
gut responses 115

Hammarskjöld, Dag 90
happiness 121, 128–9, 141–2, 148–9, 180
harm 111, 120, 146–8, 171
harmony 130, 132
    communal 129–30
healing 52, 70, 81, 89, 101, 167, 183
health 64–5, 130, 158, 165, 183
heart 22, 57, 96, 99–100, 115–16, 164, 170–2, 174
    rate 36
heartfulness 110
hell realm 146
hierarchy of needs 82
hijab 43–4
Himalayas 17, 133
Hinduism 23
history of empathy 3–45
honesty 34–5, 49, 56, 78, 81, 102, 173, 184
hopelessness 50, 101
humanity 1, 14, 50, 53, 129, 135, 174, 179–80
    common 4, 27, 34, 42–3
humanness 6–8, 14
hungry ghosts 143, 145–6
hurt 9, 22, 42, 56, 60–1, 155, 158, 160

identification 27, 31, 35
    imaginative 21, 27
identity 82
illness 18
    mental 158
images 57, 84, 110, 113, 168
    enemy 5–7, 27, 51, 135, 149
imagination 28, 35, 84, 121–2
    sense of 169
imaginative empathy 124, 171
imaginative identification 21, 27
imitation 10–11, 115, 155, 157
impermanence 112, 145
    melody of 145
independence 44
    political 50
India 23, 96, 123, 135
injury 147–8
inner world 41, 57, 72, 87, 90, 157, 167

insights, empathic 122, 145–6
integration 8, 56, 112
intellectual understanding 79, 81
intention 57, 77–9, 81, 83, 85, 91–2, 115, 120–1
    compassionate 119, 148
    ethics of 121
internal sensations 163
interoception 115
intimacy 40–1
intimate partner violence 158
investigating/interrogating 64, 71, 74
invidious comparison 123–4
Islam 23, 178
Israel 50–1, 54
Israelis 51–3, 133
Italy 114

Jainism 23
Japan 147
Jericho 24
Jerusalem 24, 52
Jesus 1, 17–29, 133
journals 74, 98–9, 101–2, 148–9, 159, 164, 166, 168
joy 28, 125
Judaism 23
judgements 7–8, 26, 45, 77, 91, 138, 149, 158–9
Jung, C.G. 112

Khan, Mohammad Sidique 177–9
Kimbila 130–1
kindness 112, 130–1; see also loving-kindness
kings 17–18, 122, 134–6, 178
Koliyans 133–6

labels 1, 34, 104, 135
language of needs 83, 119–20, 122
laughter 10
learning 11, 63, 72, 80, 88, 95, 143, 146
leisure 82, 183
liberation 42, 162
life 15, 17–20, 57–8, 60–1, 88–90, 123–4, 171–4, 179–80
    spiritual 49, 146
    taking of 124, 171
life energy 82, 181

relationships 9, 33, 35, 54–6, 82, 92, 114, 156–7
relatives 18, 133, 178
relaxation 87, 95, 100–1, 103, 109
reliability 15, 29
relief 9, 36, 95, 159
  self-righteous 27
religion 25, 27, 43–5, 119, 178–9
religious beliefs 34, 44
religious law 24–6
Remen, Rachel Naomi 94
research 23, 32, 36–40, 109, 113–14, 116, 156, 158
researchers 11–13, 36–7, 39, 114, 155
resilience 57–8, 138
resources 33, 50, 81, 104–5, 119, 133, 171–2
  inner 120
  natural 135
  shared 135
respect 29, 43–4, 61, 67, 73–4, 92, 100, 102
responsibility 27, 33, 42, 83, 120, 133, 178
restorative principles 54
rhythmic sensations 164, 166
'right' answers 14, 28, 43, 60, 125
rightdoing 77, 121, 170
Rimpoche, Dhardo 23
Rogers, Carl 32–5, 56
Rosenberg, Marshall 1, 4–7, 22, 33–4, 48–62, 66, 76–9, 86–7
Ryōkan 147–8

safety 6, 15, 41, 51–2, 55, 88, 126–7, 159
St Luke's Gospel 16, 23–4
St Matthew's Gospel 133
Śākyans 17, 133–6
salvation 19, 43
Samaritan, Good 24–6
Sangharakshita, Urgyen 23, 123–4, 170
Sanskrit 110, 131, 143
Śāntideva 140–2, 180
sati 111
satisfaction, sexual 40–1
schizophrenia 88, 153
seat belts 159–60
secure attachments 156–9
security 29, 119, 121, 156–7, 162, 174, 178, 183

inner 162
seedlings 58
self 37, 122, 142, 156
  sense of 13, 170
self-actualization 82
self-awareness 14, 18, 23, 116, 146
self-compassion 21, 57, 78, 114–16, 167, 169
self-confidence 142
self-empathy 57, 70, 77–8, 95, 138, 163, 167–70, 178–9
self-esteem 40, 73
self-expression 57, 184
selfishness 34, 56, 92, 119–20
self-respect 44, 136
self-righteous relief 27
sensations 112, 163–4, 166
  internal 163
  physical 111
  rhythmic 164, 166
sense of connection 169, 174, 180
sense of self 13, 170
sensitivity 41, 153
  ethical 23
sentient beings 21, 123, 170
sex 39–41, 119, 155, 172
sexual abuse 158
sexual communication 40
sexual ethics 171
sexual misconduct 172
sexual satisfaction 40–1
shame 52, 60
Shaw, George Bernard 24
Shelley, Percy Bysshe 27–8, 31
shock 53–5, 69, 126
sickness 18, 132–3
Siddhattha 17–19
Siegel, Dan 156–7
sights 17–19
Sikhism 23
silence 26, 36, 52, 76, 78, 94–9, 103, 105
  listening in 95–8, 103
simplicity 147, 172
sisters 134, 178
skilful awareness 121
skills 10–11, 87, 95–6, 99, 101, 122
  empathy 58, 77, 95, 169
  practical 1, 77
smiling 10–11, 113, 174
social behaviour 10, 12–13

social responsibility 42
solar plexus 56, 83, 116, 164, 166
soldiers 18, 178–9
solidarity 124, 171
South Africa 8
spiritual development 112, 147
spiritual empathy 132
spiritual life 49, 146
spiritual traditions 1, 24
sports 165
Sri Lanka 54, 133
stability 57, 183
staff 54, 89, 104, 146
states
    of consciousness 55, 131–2
    internal 163
    mental 113, 167
stillness 164, 172
stimuli 54–5
stomach 29, 56, 83, 116, 164
stories 17–22, 25, 53, 63–4, 68, 80,
    122–3, 129
strangers 133, 155
strength 13, 109, 134, 178–9
stress 39, 58, 120, 142, 147–9, 158
structure 60–1, 115, 183
subsistence 82
Suddhodana 17–18
suffering 17–18, 21–2, 51–2, 120–1,
    125, 140–2, 146–9, 179–80
suicide 154
summarizing 95–6, 99–101
support 29, 32–4, 81, 83, 110, 112–13,
    147–8, 178
surfing 79–80
surprise 5, 9, 58, 89
survival 40, 155, 183
Sutta Nipāta 124
sympathy 31, 37, 41–2, 63–4, 69–71,
    73–4, 89

Tamils 133
Taoism 23
teachers 78, 130, 141, 157
teenagers 35, 42, 54
tension 5, 29, 32, 52, 87, 164, 166, 168
terror 7–8, 52
terrorists 7–8, 53, 135, 177, 180
third-person perspective 114
Thompson, Ann 154
Thompson, Robert 154, 158

Thoreau, Henry David 108
thought experiments 113
thoughts 100–2, 109, 112–15, 126,
    137–8, 143, 162–3, 165–7
throat 116, 164, 166
Tibet 23, 143
time in 22, 90–1, 116, 167
titans 143, 145
tone of voice 56, 83, 98–9, 126, 167
tools 80, 84, 98–9, 101–2, 164, 166–7,
    180, 184
traditions, spiritual 1, 24
trainers 52, 54, 57, 88, 90
training principles 124, 169, 171–2
transcendence 82, 183
transcendental wisdom 145
Tree of Compassionate Connection
    57–9, 170
trees 20, 57–8, 134, 145
    bodhi 19, 110
trust 6, 39, 41, 77, 91, 104, 119, 158
truth 10, 19, 21, 99, 136, 147, 179, 184
turtles 155

understanding 31–2, 34, 40–1, 43–5,
    48–50, 78–9, 81–2, 177–80
    empathic 143, 145–6, 171
    mental 79
unity 35–6
unmet needs 6, 67, 77, 92
unmindfulness 65, 110, 145
upbringing 83, 154, 157

values 24, 42–3, 45, 56, 83, 119, 124,
    142
    and needs distinguished 83
vedanā 55
Venables, Jon 154, 158
victims 36–7, 154, 159
vigilance, ethical 111
violence 8, 22, 34, 37, 54, 133, 136,
    158
    intimate partner 158
    potential 76
violent films 154
Vischer, Robert 31
voice, tone of 56, 83, 98–9, 126, 167
volitions 55–6
vulnerability 26–7

walking meditation 165–6

WINDHORSE PUBLICATIONS

Windhorse Publications is a Buddhist charitable company based in the UK. We place great emphasis on producing books of high quality that are accessible and relevant to those interested in Buddhism at whatever level. We are the main publisher of the works of Sangharakshita, the founder of the Triratna Buddhist Order and Community. Our books draw on the whole range of the Buddhist tradition, including translations of traditional texts, commentaries, books that make links with contemporary culture and ways of life, biographies of Buddhists, and works on meditation.

As a not-for-profit enterprise, we ensure that all surplus income is invested in new books and improved production methods, to better communicate Buddhism in the 21st century. We welcome donations to help us continue our work – to find out more, go to windhorsepublications.com.

The Windhorse is a mythical animal that flies over the earth carrying on its back three precious jewels, bringing these invaluable gifts to all humanity: the Buddha (the 'awakened one'), his teaching, and the community of all his followers.

Windhorse Publications
169 Mill Road
Cambridge CB1 3AN
UK
info@windhorsepublications.com

Perseus Distribution
210 American Drive
Jackson TN 38301
USA

Windhorse Books
PO Box 574
Newtown NSW 2042
Australia

THE TRIRATNA BUDDHIST COMMUNITY

Windhorse Publications is a part of the Triratna Buddhist Community, an international movement with centres in Europe, India, North and South America and Australasia. At these centres, members of the Triratna Buddhist Order offer classes in meditation and Buddhism. Activities of the Triratna Community also include retreat centres, residential spiritual communities, ethical Right Livelihood businesses, and the Karuna Trust, a UK fundraising charity that supports social welfare projects in the slums and villages of India.

Through these and other activities, Triratna is developing a unique approach to Buddhism, not simply as a philosophy and a set of techniques, but as a creatively directed way of life for all people living in the conditions of the modern world.

If you would like more information about Triratna please visit thebuddhistcentre.com or write to:

London Buddhist Centre
51 Roman Road
London E2 0HU
UK

Aryaloka
14 Heartwood Circle
Newmarket NH 03857
USA

Sydney Buddhist Centre
24 Enmore Road
Sydney NSW 2042
Australia

Mindful Emotion: A Short Course in Kindness

Dr Paramabandhu Groves and Dr Jed Shamel

This book is all about kindness behaviour training (KBT). The authors have drawn on their clinical experience as well as Buddhism to develop a practical course in cultivating kindness, intended to complement and augment other mindfulness-based approaches.

A range of psychological theories and areas of research inform the KBT approach, primarily findings from cognitive neuroscience, as well as evolutionary and positive psychology literatures. It also uses a range of exercises found to be helpful in Eastern traditions, such as Buddhism. The KBT exercises have been isolated from their religious or spiritual origins and are used on a secular basis.

A stimulating guide and training program that uses the analogy of cultivating a garden that results in the finest flowers and fruits to illustrate the process of cultivating kindness toward others . . . . what our world so badly needs right now. – **Bhikshuni Thubten Chodron**

Buy this book, read it, practise with it. It's a wonderfully welcome addition to the body of work around mindfulness and compassion. I'll certainly be recommending it to all those who have attended my mindfulness classes. – **Michael Chaskalson**, author of *Mindfulness in Eight Weeks*

ISBN 978 1 909314 70 2
£11.99 / $18.95 / €14.95
240 pages

Not About Being Good: A Practical Guide to Buddhist Ethics

Subhadramati

While there are numerous books on Buddhist meditation and philosophy, there are few books that are entirely devoted to the practice of Buddhist ethics. Subhadramati communicates clearly both their founding principles and the practical methods to embody them.

Buddhist ethics are not about conforming to a set of conventions, not about 'being good' in order to gain rewards. Instead, living ethically springs from the awareness that other people are no different from yourself. You can actively develop this awareness, through cultivating love, clarity and contentment. Helping you to come into greater harmony with all that lives, this is ultimately your guidebook to a more satisfactory life.

Places ethics and meditation at the heart of Buddhist practice, and shows how they work together in transforming ordinary human beings into Buddhas. – **Professor Damien Keown**, author of *The Nature of Buddhist Ethics*

This accessible book enables the reader to understand something of Buddhist ethics through reflection and meditation; it is 'a practical guide', rejecting notions of good and bad in favour of developing awareness of the intentions that underpin actions and words. – **Joyce Miller**, *REtoday*

1SBN: 9781 909314 01 6
£9.99 / $16.95 / €12.95
176 pages

Buddhist Meditation: Tranquillity, Imagination & Insight

Kamalashila

First published in 1991, this book is a comprehensive and practical guide to Buddhist meditation, providing a complete introduction for beginners, as well as detailed advice for experienced meditators seeking to deepen their practice. Kamalashila explores the primary aims of Buddhist meditation: enhanced awareness, true happiness, and – ultimately – liberating insight into the nature of reality. This third edition includes new sections on the importance of the imagination, on Just Sitting, and on reflection on the Buddha. Kamalashila has been teaching meditation since becoming a member of the Triratna Buddhist Order in 1974. He has developed approaches to meditation practice that are accessible to people in the contemporary world, whilst being firmly grounded in the Buddhist tradition.

A wonderfully practical and accessible introduction to the important forms of Buddhist meditation. From his years of meditation practice, Kamalashila has written a book useful for both beginners and longtime practitioners. – **Gil Fronsdal,** author of *A Monastery Within*, founder of the Insight Meditation Center, California, USA

This enhanced new edition guides readers more clearly into the meditations and draws out their significance more fully, now explicitly oriented around the 'system of meditation'. This system provides a fine framework both for understanding where various practices fit in and for reflecting on the nature of our own spiritual experiences. Kamalashila has also woven in an appreciation of a view of the nature of mind that in the Western tradition is known as the imagination, helping make an accessible link to our own philosophical and cultural traditions. – **Lama Surya Das,** author of *Awakening the Buddha Within*, founder of Dzogchen Center and Dzogchen Meditation Retreats, USA

His approach is a clear, thorough, honest, and, above all, open-ended exploration of the practical problems for those new to and even quite experienced in meditation. – **Lama Shenpen Hookham**, author of *There's More to Dying Than Death,* founder of the Awakened Heart Sangha, UK

ISBN 9781 907314 09 4

£14.99 / $27.95 / €19.95

272 pages

The Buddha on Wall Street: What's Wrong with Capitalism and What We Can Do about It

Vaḍḍhaka Linn

After his Enlightenment the Buddha set out to help liberate the individual, and create a society free from suffering. The economic resources now exist to offer a realistic possibility of providing everyone with decent food, shelter, work and leisure, to allow each of us to fulfil our potential as human beings, whilst protecting the environment. What is it in the nature of modern capitalism which prevents that happening? Can Buddhism help us build something better than our current economic system, to reduce suffering and help the individual to freedom? In this thought-provoking work, Vaḍḍhaka Linn explores answers to these questions by examining our economic world from the moral standpoint established by the Buddha.

An original, insightful, and provocative evaluation of our economic situation today. If you wonder about the social implications of Buddhist teachings, this is an essential book. – **David Loy**, author *Money, Sex, War, Karma*

Lays bare the pernicious consequences of corporate capitalism and draws forth from Buddhism suggestions for creating benign alternatives conducive to true human flourishing. – **Bhikkhu Bodhi**, editor *In the Buddha's Words*

Questions any definition of wellbeing that does not rest on a firm ethical foundation, developing a refreshing Buddhist critique of the ends of economic activity. – **Dominic Houlder**, Adjunct Professor in Strategy and Entrepreneurship, London Business School

ISBN 978 1 909314 44 3
£9.99 / $16.99 / €12.95
272 pages